URBAN EDUCATIONAL IDENTITY

Through rich ethnographic detail, *Urban Educational Identity* captures the complexities of urban education by documenting the everyday practices of teaching and learning at a high-achieving, high-poverty school. Drawing on over two years of intensive fieldwork and analysis, author Sara M. Childers shows how students, teachers, and parents work both within and against traditional deficit discourses to demonstrate the challenges and paradoxes of urban schooling. It offers an up-close description of how macro-government policies are interpreted, applied, and even subverted for better or worse by students as active agents in their own education. The book moves on to develop and analyze the concept of "urban cachet," tracing how conceptions of race and class were deeply entwined with the very practices for success that propelled students towards graduation and college entrance. A poignant, insightful, and practical analysis, *Urban Educational Identity* is a timely exploration of how race and class continue to matter in schools.

Sara M. Childers is an independent scholar and Assistant Director of The Women's Place, the women's policy office, at The Ohio State University. She resides in Dublin, Ohio, USA.

The Critical Educator
Edited by Richard Delgado and Jean Stefancic

American Indian Education: Counternarratives in Racism, Struggle, and the Law
Matthew L. M. Fletcher

Foundations of Critical Race Theory in Education
Ed Taylor, David Gillborn, and Gloria Ladson-Billings

Persistent Inequality: Contemporary Realities in the Education of Undocumented Latina/o Students
Maria Pabon Lopez and Gerardo R. Lopez

Dismantling Contemporary Deficit Thinking: Educational Thought and Practice
Richard R. Valencia

Foundations of Critical Race Theory in Education, Second Edition
Ed Taylor, David Gillborn, and Gloria Ladson-Billings

Resegregation as Curriculum: The Meaning of the New Racial Segregation in U.S. Public Schools
Jerry Rosiek and Kathy Kinslow

Urban Educational Identity: Seeing Students on Their Own Terms
Sara M. Childers

URBAN EDUCATIONAL IDENTITY

Seeing Students on Their Own Terms

Sara M. Childers

Routledge
Taylor & Francis Group
NEW YORK AND LONDON

First published 2017
by Routledge
711 Third Avenue, New York, NY 10017

and by Routledge
2 Park Square, Milton Park, Abingdon, Oxon, OX14 4RN

Routledge is an imprint of the Taylor & Francis Group, an informa business

Library of Congress Cataloging in Publication Data
Names: Childers, Sara M., author.
Title: Urban educational identity : seeing students on their own terms / by Sara M. Childers.
Description: New York : Routledge, 2016. | Series: The critical educator | Includes bibliographical references and index.
Identifiers: LCCN 2016015216| ISBN 9781138842915 (hardback) | ISBN 9781138842922 (pbk.) | ISBN 9781315731247 (e-book)
Subjects: LCSH: Education, Urban—United States.
Classification: LCC LC5131 .C46 2016 | DDC 370.9173/2—dc23
LC record available at https://lccn.loc.gov/2016015216

ISBN: 978-1-138-84291-5 (hbk)
ISBN: 978-1-138-84292-2 (pbk)
ISBN: 978-1-315-73124-7 (ebk)

Typeset in Bembo
by Swales & Willis Ltd, Exeter, Devon, UK.

Printed and bound in the United States of America by Publishers Graphics, LLC on sustainably sourced paper.

To:
Ohio Magnet School,
all the teachers in my life,
and
Maizie and Vincent, who were once young enough to still call me mommy and would say to each other: "let mommy work."
And to Mark.

CONTENTS

SERIES EDITOR'S INTRODUCTION

The Critical Educator series publishes books on emerging topics in the field of education. With books on such diverse topics as Native American education, persistent inequality, deficit thinking, resegregation, and critical race theory in education, its coverage is broad. Scholars interested in submitting proposals should send a concise query letter to one of the series editors, Richard Delgado and Jean Stefancic, or supervising editor, Catherine Bernard, at her New York office.

In this volume, Sara Childers describes how children, parents, teachers, and administrators negotiated the shoals of race and class in a select urban, public high school where the student body was composed, for the most part, of low-income Black students who worked long hours at after-school jobs and struggled to stay awake in class, and ambitious white kids with middle income parents eager to enroll them in AP and IB classes. She shows how the teachers of this magnet school struggled valiantly to help them all succeed, and how students across the racial and class divides related to each other and conceptualized their futures.

The reader will learn about opportunistic parents, dedicated teachers who knew full well what they were up to but did not allow this knowledge to discourage them, and grant-writers at the school who traded on "urban cachet" to add to the school's lean budget. In an era of shrinking resources for public education and inner-city schools, confronting daily unkempt, sleepy children from troubled families, this book offers a story that is at once grim and full of hope.

Richard Delgado

ACKNOWLEDGMENTS

This book would not have been possible without the willingness of the administrators, teachers, students, and parents who allowed me to see them teach and learn. I am grateful to 'Mr. Fisher' for opening the doors and serving as a liaison early in the process, as well as for his advice and honesty. To all the teachers who welcomed me into their classrooms, I deeply admire your commitment and compassion. I learned from you what it means to meet students where they are on their own terms. And to the students, who are by now older and wiser, thank you for being open, honest, and transparent; for being teenagers unafraid to share the complexities of your lives; and for eating the donuts and pizza, and humoring me while I asked questions about this thing you do every day called school.

I also want to thank Dr. Patti Lather who advised this study as a dissertation and continued to support me as I made the transition to a book. Thank you to Antoinette Errante who provided invaluable feedback on the first version of this study as well as the proposal. I also want to thank Richard Delgado and Jean Stefancic. They provided much needed feedback on the first book proposal of this very inexperienced junior professor, and then followed it up with coffee cake and tea. I'm sorry my time at the University of Alabama was cut short, but I'm glad to have had this opportunity to work with you. My family—my sisters, Teresa Childers and Angela Colistra, my mother-in-law, Shellee Boyce, my mom, Paula Childers, and my kids, Maizie and Vincent who are now teenagers themselves—all supported me in big and small ways, without which I would not have finished. Lastly, I have a great deal of gratitude for my partner, Mark Siders, who puts up with all this academic business and keeps me grounded and calm.

1

RETHINKING URBAN EDUCATION

We'll Have "Da Bomb" Seminar: Urban Educational Identity, Agency, and Achievement

Cheering and applause erupted from the 10th grade humanities classroom in celebration of Barack Obama's election to the presidency. After a short discussion, co-teachers Mr. Fisher and Ms. Perry divided the class of 43 predominantly Black students into two groups for Socratic seminar.[1] Mr. Fisher reviewed the seminar protocol—call each other by Mr., Ms., or Miss and last name, do not interrupt, and do not shout out. I followed Mr. Fisher's group next door.

What was once an auto shop had been hollowed out to accommodate a seminar table and teacher workspaces. Old wooden desks crammed with books and overflowing with lesson plans lined the walls. I sat at a desk of an English teacher, decorated with poetry and a "reading is sexy" bumper sticker.

Students took seminar very seriously and sat at attention with their name tents, notes, and books in front of them. I was impressed with how several enthusiastically rose to the challenge of participating in this student-directed activity. Citations of Kant and Hobbes were peppered with teen slang as they referenced secondary sources to construct their arguments. Black female students dominated the 45-minute conversation, but eventually each boy made an effort to interject comments, and most of the students faithfully attempted to talk to each other and not the teacher. A tall blonde girl with pale skin and braces bravely started the discussion using the study guide, but received only stares as students processed what they wanted to say in response. Jasmine posed another argument about the text, prompting a spirited debate between Amber and Nikki who eagerly participated.

> Mr. Fisher sat quietly and offered limited prompts until it was time to wrap up, and then moved the students back to the regular classroom.
>
> "Keep it down, we're not done," he shouted over the typical talking and laughing that ensues when classrooms transition. The teachers checked students' seminar notes while the class settled. Mr. Fisher called a disheveled white girl that failed to participate to his desk. "You have all these notes, and you didn't say a thing . . . I don't understand why you don't talk in seminar." He gave the class his lecture about the importance of learning to speak in public and reiterated the goal of full participation in seminar. Nikki stated enthusiastically, already looking forward to the next one, "We'll have 'da bomb' seminar if we can get 100 percent participation."
>
> *(Field Notes, November 6, 2008)*

In the introduction to *Orientalism*, Said (1978) states that the "Orient" is an invention of the European imagination, a system of knowledge that constructs a grid through which "the Orient" and "the Occident" are understood in relation to one another. Rather than seeing this grid of knowledge as inhibiting the knowing of a "true Orient," Said argues that the persistence and sedimentation of particular hegemonic cultural frameworks demonstrate how systems of meaning constrain and produce representations of thought, living, and experience (p. 14). Using texts as representations, rather than natural depictions, Said situates the Orient as a "strategic formation" of texts and genres that "acquire mass, density, and referential power among themselves and in the culture at large" (p. 20).

I start with Said because urban educational identity might also be viewed as an "invention," a strategic formation that has gathered mass and referential power in the American psyche, that has been historically produced in and through a grid of knowledge that makes certain representations of urban schooling and student achievement possible and others difficult or (im)possible. These representations tell us more about our ways of seeing than what is represented.

The students in this vignette demonstrate the impressive levels of preparation, critical thinking, and engagement that I observed daily while conducting a two-year ethnographic case study of Ohio Magnet School (OMS).[2] These kinds of learning exchanges are generally expected of high-achieving schools. However, OMS was also designated a high-poverty lottery[3] school that served predominantly Black students from across a large urban[4] district, and it was the twin distinctions of high achievement and urban identity that brought attention from local and national media and educational organizations. When I began presenting on this study, I would share vignettes like the one above to illustrate the ways in which urban students were more than the common narratives of disadvantage, deprivation, and risk so often attributed to them. Inevitably, questions and comments about the study moved the discussion back within a grid of normalized representation in spite of the fact that I was writing against it. So ensnared by representations of the always-failing urban other, the audience would become overtaken by surprise at the success of this school, which would feed desires to romanticize the narrative, valorize the teachers, and see the students as benefactors rather than as actors invested in their own education. The romance had the effect of detracting from a discussion about the material experiences of students as they negotiated race, class, and urban identity and stalled out other ways of knowing and seeing urban education.

Its record of high achievement begged the question, why was OMS so successful when other schools demographically like it in the district and across the country were failing? But, equally, it called for an interrogation of the mechanisms that sustain urban students as objects rather than subjects of education: Why was it difficult to envision urban students as capable of such outstanding excellence on their own terms?

The Meaning and Measure of Excellence and Equity

Initially, I had intended to study OMS because it offered a critical case study of how one urban high school not only met but exceeded achievement standards when other district schools were struggling to meet minimum benchmarks. The racial and socioeconomic demographics of the student body closely mimicked the demographics of other urban schools in its district—at the time of the study 65.5 percent of the student body was Black, 27.7 percent white, 3 percent Asian or Pacific Islander, 2.5 percent Latino, and 55 percent of all students were eligible to receive free or reduced lunch. However, its high rate of academic achievement set it apart—OMS maintains an average graduation rate of 99 percent compared to the district average of 73 percent, and an average college attendance rate of 96 percent, including entrance to ivy league institutions. According to its website, recent graduates have earned over $8 million in scholarships. For these reasons, OMS continues to be recognized nationally as an urban success story. This study was an opportunity to richly document typical moments like the one that opened this chapter that offered hopeful possibilities for education.

I also became keenly aware, that while educators rightly criticized how federal policy like No Child Left Behind (NCLB) deeply undermined teaching and learning, OMS offered a rare example of a school that managed to undo policy in some powerful ways that averted the constraining effects of high-stakes testing and accountability. Therefore, this critical case study of a successful school was more complex in that the purpose was also to ethnographically document how educational polices were enacted and negotiated at the local level by analyzing the curricular and instructional practices that propelled students forward and simultaneously undercut the negative effects of NCLB. Undercutting NCLB was entwined with other practices of success.

However, policy and practice do not occur in a vacuum, but are part of the sociocultural and historical matrices of education. Whenever we are "doing" policy (i.e., engaging it as practice) we are also "doing race," (Best, 2003) or class, gender, and/or other forms of difference. Omi and Winant (2015/1986) conceptualize race "as an unstable and 'decentered' complex of social meanings constantly being transformed by political struggle" (p. 123) and define it further "*as a concept which signifies and symbolizes social conflicts and interests by referring to different types of human bodies*" (p. 123, italics theirs). They clarify this contested term arguing, "although the concept of race invokes biological based human characteristics . . . selection of these particular human features for purposes of racial signification is always and necessarily a social and historical process" (p. 123). As I discuss how schooling actors negotiated—enacted, constructed, performed, subverted, or acquiesced to—policy in and through their practice, I intend to analyze policy practices not as separate or apart from difference, but rather as constituted by and also productive of and through difference, in the case of OMS, through race and class.

Analyzing educational gains made by OMS as well as the ways in which racism and classism insidiously undermined equity provides a more complicated picture of how local school practices engender equity and excellence. I became aware of a pattern of racially stratified course enrollment and evidence of an "opportunity gap" (Milner, 2012) between white students and students of color, as basic college preparation courses enrolled predominantly Black students, and Advanced Placement and International Baccalaureate courses, perceived as more challenging and rigorous, enrolled predominantly white students. This was an aspect of OMS not discussed in news articles or state reports, but it was visibly obvious and recognized by staff as a difficult issue they largely attributed to individual student choice and coincidence. The inequity across the courses was viewed as unfortunate but easy to overlook considering that roughly 99 percent of OMS students were graduating and attending college each year.

By paying attention to the distribution of equity within the school, OMS raised questions about the meaning and measurement of excellence. What does it mean to measure excellence without consideration for equity? As we will see, in spite of this school's overt mission and its ability to close the achievement gap for its students, full equity was an elusive goal, something glimpsed but not completely realized. How might we move forward to see the necessity of including equity when assessing excellence?

Rethinking equity and excellence as mutually constitutive encourages readers to turn their gaze back on their own assumptions about the goals and actual accomplishments of national policy for students. Because of its designation as a successful urban school, OMS provides a unique opportunity to interrogate how race, class, and policy are simultaneously engaged in practices of teaching and learning. In doing so, it allows for the goals and actual "on-the-ground" gains of educational policy, beyond test scores and graduation rates, to be considered in terms of how equity is practiced and distributed inside schools. I will show that despite OMS' focus on closing the achievement gap for disadvantaged and minority students, NCLB failed as an equity reform in practice, because it elided structural inequalities and situated schooling as unburdened by discrimination or systemic disadvantage.

Lastly, OMS signals the possibilities public schooling holds for creating a climate of success that allows urban students to become academically engaged with the exploration and construction of knowledge "on their own terms," to consider them as subjects, rather than objects, of their education. I interrogate how deficit discourses of race and class were deeply entwined with the very practices of success that propelled students toward graduation and college entrance while simultaneously maintaining patterns of racial inequality and limiting access to educational opportunities within the school. Using portraits of students, I aim to see them "on their own terms." As educational subjects, rather than objects, the goal is to demonstrate how these students do not fit easily into fixed notions of urban identity that are inscribed on their raced and classed bodies. These portraits show how urban students are equally aspirational, dedicated, and committed, but that some also must navigate full-time jobs, family responsibilities, and self-care, much of which is the result of poverty and systemic inequality. By looking at how they practice themselves as educational agents, they become unfixed from rigid stereotypes, and we see that the terms of education need to be redefined to incorporate the histories, discourses, and materialities that they must negotiate.

I pose three paradoxical questions that point toward a more complex understanding of how teachers, parents, and students negotiate educational policy and urban identity: 1) What can be learned from OMS about creating a climate of success, even with limited resources, that allows students to become academically engaged with the exploration and construction of knowledge? 2) How might urban students be seen as educational subjects capable and desiring of success and achievement on their own terms? And, paradoxically, 3) How might the road paved with good intentions (and amazing test scores, graduation rates, and college entrance rates) also lead us down the path of inequality?

I have written a great deal about the methodological approach taken in this study (Childers, 2011, 2012, 2013, 2014a, 2014b; Childers, Daza, & Rhee, 2013). Theoretical and conceptual lenses are embedded within the chapters, however, the next section is a synopsis that addresses the theoretical frameworks of Critical Race Theory, Foucault, and Derrida brought to bear on my thinking with the empirical materials and how they influenced the "policy as practice" (Sutton & Levinson, 2001) methodology. The remainder of this chapter will then explain the organization of the book. A full nuts and bolts description of the research design is located in Appendix I at the end of the book.

Methodology

OMS was a popular school, and many colleagues and faculty that I knew in the university community had children who attended there or had attempted to get in but had not been lucky in the lottery. My interest was piqued by 2007, and I began to build relationships with parents and teachers as I learned more about this high-profile school. In 2008 I officially began a two-year ethnographic case study that included observations, interviews, focus groups, and document analysis. I carried out 9 consecutive months of fieldwork in a school of over 600 students, visiting the school 3 or 4 days a week and spending anywhere from 3 to 6 hours observing and interviewing. I interviewed 40 students, teachers, administrators, and parents, and I compiled an archive of over 50 policy and non-policy documents including reports, websites, news articles, press releases, yearbooks, and curriculum materials. My fieldwork continued when I was invited back in December of 2009, at which point I had the opportunity to conduct three member checks with different constituents and participants.

Success at OMS was deeply entwined with inequity. In fact, the identity of this "successful urban school" hinged on deficit notions of students of color as the always-failing and at risk as opposed to educational agents who were responsible for their own achievement. What sustained the school's reputation was the surprise that such graduation and college-going rates were possible at an urban (i.e., Black and poor) school. Simultaneously, these deficit discourses subtly permeated academic advising and student scheduling in a ghostly counterbalance to the climate of high achievement that filled the school.

But this was not an either/or story. Students were graduating and attending college at rates higher than any other school in the district, and this had huge implications for their futures. Students spoke at great length about how they were positively impacted. They discussed how they felt challenged and supported in ways they would not have been at traditional schools in the district and how the climate of high expectations instilled in them a sense of pride. And almost in the same breath, some would explain how they had been excluded or persuaded not to pursue an academic opportunity.

In spite of its best intentions to harness educational excellence as a way to promote and sustain educational equity, OMS also perpetuated inequality even while its students were for all intents and purposes closing the achievement gap. While policy ethnography became my way into the complicated story, I realized that a multi-methodological and theoretical approach was needed to work the disruptions of (un)success rather than forfeit them for the sake of a cohesive narrative about the school (Childers, 2011). The data disrupted any one way of seeing, and the methodology needed to follow the disruptive energy rather than try to tame it.

I found Critical Race Theory (CRT) and the theoretical approaches of Foucault and Derrida, when worked together, to be the most helpful in bringing forth the complexities in spite of their assumed or prescribed incommensurability (Childers, 2014a). Any one theory, concept, or framework alone seemed unsuited to get at the nuances of how race worked materially and discursively in this school, but when I thought about the data with these theories simultaneously, the disruptions remained in play because these theories were critical and disruptive of each other. Rather than fear what it meant to transgress methodological prescription, I began to think about my approach to theory and methodology as "promiscuous" (Childers, Daza, & Rhee, 2013)—as a way to think through the dangers of incommensurability and allow methodological and theoretical promiscuity to push the limits of knowing, make interventions, and help the study thrive on the tensions, complications, and losses of research in ways that might be productive.

Curriculum and Instruction as Policy as/in Practice

Disrupting traditional approaches to policy analysis is not new (see Marshall, 1997; Pillow, 2004; Scheurich, 1994, 1997). Researchers seeking to recognize the local complexities of policy have previously adopted methodological frameworks like policy ethnography, feminist critical analysis, and poststructural policy analysis.

Sutton and Levinson (2001) call for an on-the-ground engagement with educational policy that elucidates the "richness and complexity of the policy process" to see the way policy works as a cultural practice (p. 4), with particular attention paid to "*policy as a practice of power*" (p. 1). Foucaultian theories of power/knowledge (1977) and discourse were therefore embedded in a sociocultural approach to policy analysis. Michel Foucault's theories of the relationship between power and knowledge assert that:

> (p)ower produces knowledge; that Power and knowledge directly imply one another that there is no power relation without the correlative constitution of a field of knowledge, nor any knowledge that does not presuppose and constitute at the same time power relations.
>
> *(Foucault, 1977, p. 27)*

This notion of power/knowledge as "everywhere . . . unbalanced, heterogeneous, unstable, and tense" (Foucault, 1990, p. 93) is embedded in the idea of policy as practice. Policies therefore are power/knowledge. Looking at policies as practices of power shifts the analysis from the macro-process of policy development and implementation planning to policy-on-the ground, the micro-level engagements of schooling actors with institutional policies, and the effects of these local practices of policy appropriation in schools. In effect, it shifts to consider policy as a discursive practice with limits and ruptures.

I use Foucault's theories of discourse to shift thinking to how power/knowledge shapes practice. According to Sara Mills (2004/1997), Foucault offers three different ways to think of discourse:

> [u]tterances or texts which have meaning and which have some effects in the real world . . . discourses, that is groups of utterances which seem to

> be regulated in some way and which seem to have a coherence and a force to them in common . . . [and] the rules and structures which produce particular utterances and texts.
>
> (*p. 6*)

St. Pierre (2000) continues, "Foucault's theory of discourse illustrates how language gathers itself together according to socially constructed rules and regularities that allow certain statements to be made and not others" (p. 485). Because it looks for historical shifts when people do or say things differently, it also looks at the productive nature of discourse within fields of power/knowledge and possibilities for resistance. In these ways, Foucaultian theories become useful for tracing how discourses of urban schooling and students are produced in and through policy, and productive of the practices/effects documented in this study.

Simply put, policies are "things that set limits" (Frederick Erickson cited in Bridges, Smeyers, & Smith, 2009, p. 161). Levinson, Sutton, and Winstead (2009) unpack ways to define policy, contrasting a traditional or normative definition and a critical, socially theorized definition of policy as a practice of power. Policy as traditionally defined represents a set of normative guidelines often in the form of an authorized, governing text or document that codifies appropriate behaviors and responses to the policy (p. 768). This is the definition operationalized by mainstream educational policy research.

Socially theorized policy is multi-dimensional, and the taken-for-granted positioning of policy as mere mandate is disrupted by the recognition of policy as action, production, practice, discourse, and power. Policy is viewed as an "on-going social practice of normative cultural production constituted by diverse actors across diverse contexts" (Levinson, Sutton, & Winstead, 2009, p. 770). Much like Foucault's discursive practice, rather than a static thing or text, policy is a "practice" or "process" through which life and behavior become authorized by people or groups across social contexts. As such, policy can be authorized, somehow legally binding either by law or force, or unauthorized, developed informally in networks outside of institutions invested with the power of official policy-making. Policy therefore does not have to be a text or document; it can also exist as a form of practice and institutional memory. The act of writing policy can itself be viewed as one of many policy practices. Power is located within the "will to policy," a set of conditions that make policy (authorized, unauthorized, as a practice, or a text) possible and also the "will in policy," the matrix of competing and overlapping power relations that permeate the social field through which power as policy flows (Levinson, Sutton, & Winstead, 2009, pp. 770–778).

Traditional policy studies have focused on policy implementation as an investigation of operating procedures prescribed by policy that either did or did not produce the intended results. Levinson et al. (2009) disrupt this traditional evaluation of implementation to foreground how social practice shapes policy via *formation*, *negotiation*, and *appropriation*:

1. *Formation* looks at how policy problems become socially and politically normalized or produced within and as normative cultural discourses.
2. *Negotiation* is about meaning-making and the socially contingent process through which meaning is negotiated and mobilized.
3. *Appropriation* takes the place of implementation in understanding how policy circulates in and through the social field at later stages of the policy process. It is the way creative agents take in and interpret policy and incorporate it into their social worlds. It is sense-making as/in practice, and opens up the possibility for resistance and agency through local re-appropriations of authorized policy as new and maybe unauthorized forms of practice. All of these processes are marked by an on-going process of mutual engagement by diverse actors across diverse social arenas (Levinson et al., 2009, pp. 778–779).

In relation to my study, the policy as practice framework worked synergistically with Foucaultian theory to elucidate how policy as power circulated in schools and was lived by participants, and also helped me to see how curriculum and instruction were discursive practices shaped by policy and social context. But utilizing only Foucaultian theories as an analytic framework reinforced a discursive analysis that I found on its own to be insufficient to engage the way race produced structural inequalities for Black students and other students of color. It was not that a policy as practice framework or Foucaultian analysis excluded attention to race, but it did not provide the explanatory power needed to address directly the complex lived experiences of participants. As I explore in the next section, it was necessary to bring a critical race approach to this methodology.

The Missing Discourse of Race in Policy Analysis

In a special issue of *Race Ethnicity and Education* (Leonardo, 2007b) contributors argued that the NCLB policy in and of itself is a racial project, not merely a set of policies aimed at closing the achievement gap, but policies heavily invested in the larger racial system of the United States. The editor boldly asserted:

> Overtly, it implicates improvements for students of color . . . Implicitly, NCLB is part of a racial project since it is enacted within a racialized nation-state. As part of the racialized state apparatuses, schools bear the markings and carry the anxieties of US race relations.
>
> *(Leonardo, 2007a, p. 241)*

These researchers charged that NCLB ignored the structural inequalities of the education system perpetuated in and through the racial system of the United States. Furthermore, Tyack remarked previously that "policy talk about questions of diversity in education today often ignores a long history of the social and political constructions of difference in American society and public schools" (1993, p. 8).

The policy as practice framework and Foucaultian theories did not directly address the anxieties of race relations or the material realities of Black and other students of color at OMS. My training in qualitative inquiry focused a great deal on the crisis of representation and the potential violences of research. The complications of "writing culture" (Clifford & Marcus, 1986), "racing research and researching race" (Twine & Warren, 2000), and extremely complex critiques of research and poststructuralism made by feminists of color such as Patricia Hill-Collins (2000/1990), Gloria Anzaldua (1999/1987), bell hooks (1981), and many others forced me to consider the insufficiency of using only Foucaultian theory to try to address the materiality of students' lives.

Racialized enrollment at OMS was not just a discursive practice to be analyzed. While this was a study of local policy in practice, the local was also a materiality sustained by and further sustaining of long-term historical and social structural inequalities based on race. It had material effects on students' ability to access opportunities, such as Black students' limited access to Advanced Placement and International Baccalaureate courses in high school that could later offset college expenses and time-to-degree upon entering post-secondary education. To understand the process of policy negotiation at the local level, I needed to be accountable methodologically to directly addressing the "real" racial inequalities experienced by students, naming how white privilege was bound up in these inequalities, and rendering visible the logics of the practices. CRT in education (Ladson-Billings & Tate, 1995) provided a way to engage the missing discourse of race in policy analysis.

CRT emerged in the early 1970s out of the field of critical legal studies in response to the stalled pace of successful civil rights litigation and legal reform intended to dismantle racial discrimination practices in housing, schooling, and hiring. According to Taylor (2009, p. 2):

> [f]rustrated by this backlash, and the perceived failure of traditional civil rights theories and methods, a group of legal scholars including Derrick A. Bell, Charles Lawrence, Richard Delgado, Lani Guinier, and Kimberle Crenshaw, began to openly criticize the role of law in the construction and maintenance of racially based social and economic oppression. They also began looking for an explanation of why this seeming retraction occurred, and how to formulate new strategies to affect transformation.

Crenshaw, Gotanda, Peller, and Thomas (1995) in their foundational text identified six unifying themes. CRT:

- recognizes racism as endemic to our life and society;
- challenges dominant legal claims of neutrality, objectivity, colorblindness, and meritocracy;
- argues against ahistoricism and insists that law must be analyzed within history and context;

- locates its analysis within the experiential knowledge of people of color and privileges this type of knowledge through the use of narrative and storytelling;
- is interdisciplinary;
- views activism and social change as requisite components of its work toward the elimination of racial oppression and the larger goal of ending all forms of oppression (Matsuda, Lawrence, Delgado, & Crenshaw, 1993, cited in Dixson & Rousseau, 2006, p. 33).

Ladson-Billings and Tate (1995) applied CRT specifically to education and argued that though race is deeply implicated in US society and the US educational system, it remained under-theorized in educational research. They offered three propositions from which analysis of social inequity using CRT in education might proceed: 1) race continues to be a significant factor in determining inequity in the US; 2) US society is based on property rights; and 3) the intersection of race and property creates an analytic tool through which we can understand social and consequently school inequity (p. 48). CRT in education critically addresses issues related to the achievement gap, deficit thinking, policy, higher education, school sports, curriculum and instruction, teacher education, to educational issues beyond desegregation.

CRT provides this study with the conceptual power to name and trace the way race works in schools. Race is an inescapable problematic that takes shape within the historical, social, and discursive contexts of US education. CRT in education explicitly names and defines practices of racism and white privilege, and holds this study accountable to consciously addressing racialized practices of schooling theoretically and substantively. I found, however, that CRT alone could not open the study up to students' varied practices and understandings of achievement and success or to the complex negotiations that produced urban students as subjects, rather than objects, of education.

Seeing Students on Their Own Terms

The urban educational other is the binary counterpart to the white, privileged, successful student. In the current moment, it is also other to itself. The term "urban" has become a generic and de-raced signifier attempting to hide its reliance on race, but race functions in meaningful ways. "Urban" students, their raced bodies, and what they euphemistically stand for become useful in showcasing successful urban schools like OMS and their transformative effects on "the disadvantaged."

I use the terms *subject* and *object* to mark "urban" as a practice of the subject or as a tool for identification of the "urban" object. Belsey (1997) discusses the subject within ideology through Althusser's concept of "interpellation" (1971, p. 174) to talk about processes of identity and subjectivity together. Interpellation is "the process of constituting concrete individuals as subjects"

(p. 171) through ideological frameworks and pre-existing identities in formation. In one sense, urban students are "hailed" or acknowledged and named as a particular identity with a particular set of traits which makes them instantly categorizable and locates them within subject positions that are culturally and historically situated. However, this process of interpellation is one outside of the agency of the subject. It's a naming that comes from elsewhere and positions the individual in this transaction as an object. According to Althusser, "individuals are always-already subjects" (p. 180) in that they are always enmeshed in processes of identity. Subjectivity becomes a site of action, a place where it is "linguistically and discursively constructed and displaced across a range of discourses in which the concrete individual participates" (Belsey, 1997, p. 596). Poststructuralism opens up the category of the subject "to the possibility of continual reconstruction and reconfiguration" (St. Pierre, 2000, p. 502), and I want to harness this potential for thinking about urban students as agents in their own education. Rather than objects of only interpellation, I want to look at their energy of subjectivity and the ways in which urban students resist and redefine themselves as urban educational subjects on their own terms.

Student "agency" happens within the constraints of discourse, but it is through the "subversive repetition" (Butler, 1993) of subjectivity through lived experience, or the process of repeating identities but in ways that are unfaithful, off course, and exceeding the constraints of power and knowledge that other ways of living, thinking, and doing become possible. This study locates places where urban identity categories fall apart in practice, where students work within discourses that produce and are productive of conditions that make it possible for them to claim achievement.

Deconstruction prompts us to think about how the proper term, or identity, *urban* holds within its folds many silences, absences, and impossibilities, opening up the signifier of urban identity to the radical alterity of the urban educational subject. According to Derrida and Caputo (1997), deconstruction is:

> [a] more "productive," fine-grained, distinctly deconstructive reading, which explores the tensions, loose threads, the little "openings" in the text which the classical reading tends to close over or put off as a problem for another day, which is really just a way to forget them.
>
> *(p. 76)*

I am interested in these loose threads and little openings for their potential to see students differently. This conceptual framework makes room for the complications and disruptions in the empirical materials that challenged the common narratives of urban students to reconsider them as *urban educational subjects on their own terms.*

The idea of deconstruction as a method is often eschewed for broader interpretations that would be considered more loyal to Derrida's philosophical ideas.

Derrida, himself resistant to the potential closure of philosophy through assertions of method that posit a *knowing* subject capable of *doing* deconstruction, is emphatic that "deconstruction is not a method and cannot be transformed into one, especially if the technical and procedural significations of the words are stressed" (1991, p. 273). Rather, "Deconstruction takes place, it is an event that does not await deliberation, consciousness or organization of a subject, or even of modernity. *It deconstructs it-self. It can be deconstructed*" (p. 274). The hope of "deconstruction" is its forever-open and unlimited ontological possibility.

Yet Spivak (1997)[5] does her readers a great service momentarily slipping between deconstruction as method and deconstruction as (im)possible. According to Spivak, a deconstructive reader "devotes his attention to the text in its margins . . . he examines the minute particulars of an undecidable moment, nearly imperceptible displacements, that might otherwise escape the reader's eye" (p. lxxvi). More than just a reversal and displacement of binary oppositions, deconstruction offers a way:

> [t]o locate the promising marginal text, to disclose its undecidable moment, to pry it loose with the positive lever of the signifier; to reverse the resident hierarchy, only to displace it; to dismantle in order to reconstitute what is always already inscribed. Deconstruction in a nutshell. But take away the assurance of the text's authority, the critic's control, and the primacy of meaning, and the possession of this formula does not guarantee much.
>
> *(p. lxxvii)*

Spivak makes clear that deconstruction "can never be a positive science" (p. lxxviii); an interminable, impossible act that is always under erasure, "deconstruction deconstructs deconstruction" (p. lxxvii). Deconstruction then becomes situated as a pseudo-methodology, one that posits (im)possible practices and ways of reading, and simultaneously disavows deconstruction as a method that one can "do."

Biesta (2009) urges us to bear witness to the event of deconstruction that is always already on the move. For Biesta, the act of witnessing promotes a quasi-transcendental position that undoes "the traditional philosophical gesture in which the philosopher positions himself on some safe ground outside of the scene of analysis" (p. 392). He argues that the end of deconstruction as method creates the possibility for a different relationship with deconstruction, that of "witnessing" it as affirmative event of the other. According to Biesta:

> What is at stake in witnessing metaphysics-in-deconstruction is an affirmation of what is wholly other, of what is unforeseeable from the present. It is as Derrida puts it, an affirmation of an otherness that is always to come, as an event that "as event, exceeds calculation, rules, programs, anticipations," (Derrida, 1992, p. 27) . . . In some places Derrida refers to this as "the impossible." For Derrida "the impossible" is not what is *im*possible but what cannot be foreseen as a possibility.

Deconstruction is a provocative approach for bearing witness to the materialities of urban students, because their lives exceed shallow assumptions, and we need analytic techniques that do more than dictate static identities, fixed patterns, and seamless narratives to validate inquiry. Deconstruction as an analytic move facilitates an opportunity to witness the unstable and productive event of subjectivity that unhinges students from deficit discourses, to witness the "destabilizing, rupturing process of displacement or inversion," and welcome the "undoing and unraveling" (Tarc, 2005, p. 839) as an affirmative response to these participants.

There are two specific concepts from Derrida's writing that I used to think through these issues of urban subjectivity. Through the concept of *différance*, deconstruction prompts a destabilization of the potential for this study to sustain an unproblematic urban identity or reaffirm the essentialized urban signifier in uncomplicated ways. *Différance*[6] is an engagement with what differs and defers (Derrida, 1997, p. 23), a metaphysical idea we might use "to explain how the meaning of language shifts depending on social context so that meaning can always be disputed" (St. Pierre, 2000, p. 481). It is identified as the "trace or track of all that is not what is being defined or posited" (Spivak, 1999, p. 424) that disrupts the restricted binary formulations and transgresses the imposed boundaries of knowledge. As will be seen in upcoming chapters, the idea of *différance* allowed me think against closed narratives of *urban educational identity*, but also to place them "under erasure," or to recognize the material realities of students without tying them down to the deficit discourses that are entangled with them.

Yet as I worked against the constant resurrection of the *urban other*, I also acknowledged the equally damaging possibility of delegitimating the lived experiences of systemic poverty and racial oppression that do indeed impact students in urban schools. This is one paradox this study inhabited, of how to legitimate the materiality of urban schooling for students and teachers without closing the opportunity to witness what is wholly other, unforeseeable, and always to come.

In recognizing the representation of these students as places of doubt in my work, deconstruction required persistent reflexivity that forced me to be "acutely sensitive to the contingency of our constructions, to the deeply historical, social, and linguistic 'constructedness' of our beliefs and practices" (Derrida & Caputo, 1997, p. 52). This study was an incomplete attempt to see them as agents on their own terms. I could not completely and fully comprehend or rightly represent them in this text, therefore this work presents "an impossible passage, undecidable moment, and unaccomplishable task; an event that does not pass, but remains in the coming of the other" (Derrida, 1993, p. 8).

The mere recognition of damaging discourses and the admission of such potential "bias" is not enough to counterbalance transgressions that may cloud interpretations. Derrida's work allows me to stay attuned to the fact that a mere attentiveness to historical constructions will not save me from politics of (mis)representation or get me off the hook. Rather than asserting a coming to know, I assert unknowing where students simultaneously inhabit, re-appropriate, and puncture the containment of urban identity.

I relied on stories of participants to locate and analyze the singular, disloyal, and unstable subjectivities in play and the places where possibility and impossibility crossed and provided a deconstructive opening (Biesta, 2009). What can be powerful about ethnographic research is the potential to witness living anew. I argue that theory can help qualitative research(ers) be better positioned to accept the loose threads, tensions, complete breaks, small cracks, or subtle slippages in what we think we know about our participants—if we are willing to risk simple practices and findings for more nuanced, unsteady, and even fleeting glimpses of what we document in the field.

Organization of Chapters

The remainder of the book is organized as follows:

Chapter 2 sketches the "troubled legacy" (Anderson, 2006) of the *Brown v Board of Education* (1954) decision and its impact on the Columbus City School District to dynamically interrogate how OMS came to be positioned as an "urban" school. By looking at this history, it interrupts the dominant deficit discourses that surround the notion of urban by demonstrating how *success*, *excellence*, and *achievement* were *always*, *already* at work in Black public education in Columbus prior to *Brown*. Bringing the troubled legacy of *Brown* and the history of Black education back into focus, this further reconceptualizes urban students as educational subjects on their own terms.

Chapter 3 takes an in-depth look at how the culture of high expectations was sustained in spite of the heavy hand of educational policy. I argue that by offering *only* college preparatory courses within a culture of high expectations, OMS appeared to be re-appropriating NCLB policies in ways that undid some of the constraining effects of accountability, like "teaching to the test." OMS redefined accountability on its own terms through the higher standards of an all-inclusive college prep curriculum that incorporated Advanced Placement and International Baccalaureate programs. And students rose to the challenge. However, the second part of the chapter disrupts the idea that OMS was completely above the effects of NCLB. Columbus City Schools was a failing district that struggled to raise graduation rates and test scores, and, as such, OMS was not immune from district initiatives to do so. This chapter critiques two initiatives, test preparation and credit recovery, and the ways in which participants felt punished and exploited both in spite of the school's success, and because of its success.

Chapter 4 looks at the racialized practices of enrollment that created opportunity gaps within the school. By tracing discourses of disadvantage, color blindness, and student choice, we see how inequality was justified and how the construction of urban students within these damaging discourses allowed the school to overlook structural issues that may have impeded students' ability and desire to enroll in upper level course opportunities.

Chapter 5 introduces the concept of 'urban cachet.' In its transformation from predominantly white desegregation-era magnet school to predominantly Black urban success story, OMS developed a kind of 'urban cachet,' or prestige and uniqueness because of its urban-ness. This chapter looks at three examples of urban cachet and the effects of appropriating urban identity, and interrogates the productive effects of that cachet for increasing resources by objectifying students.

Chapter 6 exposes the micro-level identity constructions of students at OMS. 'Those students' and 'successful students' were rigid local discursive positions sustained by raced and classes representations of urban identity that created a binary through which students were filtered and categorized. I critique the effects of these identity formations on everyday teaching and learning at OMS and the real life implications this process of categorization had for students.

Chapter 7 is the conclusion to the book and offers portraits of three students at OMS and the perspectives of two amazing teachers. They represent the ways in which students did not fit neatly into either category of the "successful student" or "those students," and through the materiality of their lives disrupted limiting representations of themselves as disadvantaged, disinterested, or disengaged. Viewed through the lenses of their lives both inside and outside of school, they demonstrate how they are agents invested in their own educations as they navigate life circumstances and structural inequalities while making proactive decisions about their educational success. They offer an opportunity to re-envision them as urban educational subjects on their own terms.

Unconventional Conventions

Between the chapters, there are vignettes to contextualize the study and offer more depth. The affective experience of witnessing first hand teaching and learning at OMS, sitting in the seats, surrounded by the students, their energy, and their conversations, greatly shaped my analytic work. This witnessing produced tensions, marked the moments of contradiction, and drove my analysis. To stylistically capture the materiality of the experience and share the richness of the school and its students that propelled me, I have interspersed narrative vignettes between the chapters to attempt to convey the vibrancy and fullness of the field site, as well as to provide lived stories of contradiction to unsettle simple understandings of life in this school. I recognize these vignettes may interrupt the ability to read with linearity, but the goal is to utilize interruptions and complexities to keep the study open to other ways of seeing and doing.

As is common in ethnographies, I include a short reflexive section in Appendix I that addresses the research design and my positionality. I discuss some of the methodological decisions that were made as the study shifted as well as the ethical issues I ran up against.

Lastly, Appendix II provides a set of recommendations. After administrators and parents invited me back to share what I learned, the school's principal focused on changing the racial tracking pattern, and the school requested recommendations based on the study for addressing this issue.

Notes

1 When I observed in classrooms, I would count the number of students and assess visually a racial and gender breakdown. While relying solely on this phenotypic assumption of race and gender was highly problematic and did not account for self-identity, the count allowed me to paint a picture for the reader of what the class "looked like." Though this school was predominantly Black, not all courses shared the same demographic breakdown. They became "whiter" as the courses were deemed more rigorous. On this day in 10th grade social studies, there were 27 Black females, 18 Black males, 1 Asian American male, 5 white females, and 2 white males.

2 Pseudonyms were used to protect the identity of the school and participants. I do not use a pseudonym for the district, because historical sources and documents identify it by name. Also, I do not provide references for websites, news articles, or press releases as they include the name of the school and would therefore jeopardize confidentiality.

3 As part of the choice initiative under NCLB, Columbus City Schools created a lottery process that allowed students to complete an application that placed them in a "lottery" to attend schools of their choosing. Students are randomly "drawn out of a hat" for enrollment. OMS typically has close to 1,000 lottery applicants each year vying for 150 freshman seats.

4 OMS was designated by the Ohio Department of Education (ODE) as a "high-achieving, high-poverty" urban school located in a Major Urban District. It has been recognized each year as an Urban School of Promise by ODE since 2004. The percentages of students of color and economically disadvantaged students fluctuate each year.

5 See also Lather (2007) and Derrida and Caputo (1997) for further methodological insights.

6 My treatment here is admittedly simplified. See Derrida (1991, pp. 63–79) for a more encompassing discussion of the idea.

References

Althusser, L. (1971). Ideology and ideological state apparatuses. In L. Althusser, (Ed.), *Lenin and Philosophy and Other Essays* (pp. 127–188). (B. Brewster, Trans.). London: New Left Books.

Anderson, J. D. (October 01, 2006). A tale of two "Browns": Constitutional equality and unequal education. *Yearbook of the National Society for the Study of Education, 105*(2), 14–35.

Anzaldua, G. (1999/1987). *Borderlands, La Frontera: The New Mestiza* (2nd ed.). San Francisco, CA: Aunt Lute Books.

Belsey, K. (1997). Constructing the subject, deconstructing the text. In R. Warhol and D. Herndi (Eds.), *Feminisms: An Anthology of Literary Theory and Criticisms* (pp. 657–673). New Brunswick, NJ: Rutgers University Press.

Best, A. (2003). Doing race in the context of feminist interviewing: Constructing whiteness through talk. *Qualitative Inquiry, 9*(6), 895–914.

Biesta, G. (2009). Witnessing deconstruction in education: Why quasi-transcendentalism matters. *Journal of Philosophy of Education, 43*(3), 391–404.

Bridges, D., Smeyers, P., & Smith, R. (Eds.). (2009). *Evidence-Based Education Policy: What Evidence? What Basis? Whose Policy?* Sussex, UK: Wiley-Blackwell.

Brown v. Board of Education of Topeka, 347 U.S. 483. (1954).

Butler, J. (1993). *Bodies That Matter: On the Discursive Limits of "Sex."* New York: Routledge.

Childers, S. M. (2011). Getting in trouble: Feminist post-critical policy ethnography in an urban school. *Qualitative Inquiry, 17*(5), 345–354.

Childers, S. M. (2012). Against simplicity, against ethics: Analytics of disruption as quasi-methodology. *Qualitative Inquiry, 18*(9), 752–761.

Childers, S. M. (2013). The materiality of fieldwork: Ontology of feminist becoming. *International Journal of Qualitative Studies in Education, 26*(5), 598–602.

Childers, S. M. (2014a). Promiscuous methodology: Breaching the limits of theory and practice for a social science we can live with. In R. Brown, R. Carducci, and C. Kuby, *Disrupting Qualitative Inquiry: Possibilities and Tensions in Educational Research.* New York: Peter Lang.

Childers, S. M. (2014b) Promiscuous analysis in qualitative research. *Qualitative Inquiry, 20*(6), 819–826.

Childers, S. M., Daza, S. L., & Rhee, J. (Eds.) (2013). Editors' introduction. *International Journal of Qualitative Studies in Education, 26*(5), 507–523.

Clifford, J. & Marcus, G. E. (1986). *Writing Culture: The Poetics and Politics of Ethnography.* Berkeley, CA: University of California Press.

Crenshaw, K., Gotanda, N., Peller, G., & Thomas, K. (Eds.). (1995). *Critical Race Theory: The Key Writings That Formed the Movement.* New York: The New Press.

Derrida, J. (1991). Letter to a Japanese friend. In J. Derrida and P. Kamuf (Eds.), *A Derrida Reader: Between the Blinds* (pp. 20–27). New York: Columbia University Press.

Derrida, J. (1992). Force of law: The "mystical foundation of authority." In D. Cornell, M. Rosenfeld and D. Carlson (Eds.), *Deconstruction and the Possibility of Justice* (pp. 3–67). London: Routledge.

Derrida, J. (1993). *Aporias: Dying-Awaiting (One Another at) the "Limits of Truth"* (mourir-s'attendre aux "limites de la vérité"). Stanford, CA: Stanford University Press.

Derrida, J. (1997). *De la Grammatologie* (Of grammatology). Baltimore, MD: Johns Hopkins University Press. (Original work published 1976).

Derrida, J. & Caputo, J. D. (1997). *Deconstruction in a Nutshell: A Conversation with Jacques Derrida.* New York: Fordham University Press.

Dixson, A. D. & Rousseau, C. K. (Eds.) (2006). *Critical Race Theory in Education: All God's Children Got a Song.* New York: Routledge.

Foucault, M. (1977). *Discipline and Punish: The Birth of the Prison.* New York: Vintage Books.

Foucault, M. (1990). *The History of Sexuality: An Introduction* (Vol. 1, R. Hurley, Trans.). New York: Vintage.

Hill-Collins, P. (2000/1990). *Black Feminist Thought: Knowledge, Consciousness, and the Politics of Empowerment.* New York: Routledge.

hooks, b. (1981). *Ain't I a Woman: Black Women and Feminism.* New York: South End Press.

Ladson-Billings, G. & Tate, W. F. (1995). Toward a critical race theory of education. *Teachers College Record, 97*(1), 47–68.

Lather, P. (2007). *Getting Lost: Feminist Efforts toward a Doubled Science.* Albany, NY: State University of New York Press.

Leonardo, Z. (2007a). The war on schools: NCLB, nation creation and the educational construction of whiteness. *Race Ethnicity and Education, 10*(3), 261–278.

Leonardo, Z. (Ed.). (2007b). Special issue on No Child Left Behind (Special issue). *Race Ethnicity and Education, 10*(3).

Levinson, B. A. U., Sutton, M., & Winstead, T. (2009). Education policy as a practice of power: Theoretical tools, ethnographic methods, democratic options. *Educational Policy, 23*(6), 767–795.

Marshall, C. (Ed.). (1997). *Feminist Critical Policy Analysis I: A Perspective from Primary and Secondary Schooling* (Vol. 1). London: The Falmer Press.

Matsuda, M., Lawrence, C., Delgado, R., & Crenshaw, K. (Eds.). (1993). *Words that Wound: Critical Race Theory, Assaultive Speech, and the First Amendment.* Boulder, CO: Westview.

Mills, S. (2004/1997). *Discourse.* New York: Routledge.

Milner, H. R. (2012). Beyond a test score: Explaining opportunity gaps in educational practice. *Journal of Black Studies, 43*(6), 693–718.

No Child Left Behind Act, 20 U.S.C. § 6301, (2001).

Omi, M. & Winant, H. (2015/1986). *Racial Formation in the United States.* New York: Routledge.

Pillow, W. (2004). *Unfit Subjects: Educational Policy and the Teen Mother.* New York: RoutledgeFalmer.

Said, E. (1978). *Orientalism.* New York: Pantheon.

Scheurich, J. J. (1994). Policy archeology: A new policy studies methodology. *Educational Policy, 9*(4), 297–316.

Scheurich, J. J. (1997). *Research Method in the Postmodern.* London: Falmer.

Spivak, G. C. (1997). Translator's preface. In J. Derrida, *Of Grammatology* (pp. ix–lxxxviii). Cambridge, MA: Harvard University Press.

Spivak, G. C. (1999). Appendix: The setting to work of deconstruction. In G. C. Spivak, *A Critique of Postcolonial Reason: Toward a History of the Vanishing Present* (pp. 423–431). Cambridge, MA: Harvard University Press.

St. Pierre, E. A. (2000). Poststructural feminism in education: An overview. *International Journal of Qualitative Studies in Education, 13*(5), 477–515.

Sutton, M., & Levinson, B. A. U. (Eds.). (2001). *Policy as Practice: Toward a Comparative Sociocultural Analysis of Educational Policy.* Westport, CT: Ablex.

Tarc, A. M. (December 01, 2005). Education as humanism of the other. *Educational Philosophy and Theory, 37*(6), 833–849.

Taylor, E. (2009). The foundations of critical race theory in education: An introduction. In E. Taylor, D. Gillborn, and G. Ladson-Billings (Eds.), *Foundations of Critical Race Theory in Education* (pp. 1–13). New York: Routledge.

Twine, F. W. & Warren, J. (Eds.) (2000). *Racing Research, Researching Race.* New York: University Press.

Tyack, D. B. (1993). Constructing difference: Historical reflections on schooling and social diversity. *Teachers College Record, 95*(1), 8–34.

WILL I GET INTO TROUBLE?

Negotiating the Terms of Research

I have a contact at the high school, a teacher I'll call Mr. Fisher, who has been extremely helpful in gaining access to the site. He asked me to meet him at a 50s style donut shop by the university on what turns out to be one of those crisp spring Ohio mornings. He has offered to pave the way for my formal entry into the school for data collection and wants to have a better understanding of my project.

We get cups of the world's strongest coffee and warm donuts. I don't do caffeine, but decaf doesn't exist in this place; between the sugar and coffee I feel jittery and alert, but it shakes the morning cobwebs out of my brain. Mr. Fisher is extremely gracious, friendly, and gruff at the same time, so we practically forego the formalities and how are yous, which I do not mind. I have never been good at small talk. I outline my project: I'm interested in how schools negotiate policy in the face of No Child Left Behind to promote academic achievement and engagement when other schools are complaining about teaching to the test; the impact of race on social constructions of achievement, namely why we are so surprised when students of color achieve; and the impact of high school sports on academic success since this school has no sports program.

He's straightforward and I learn some useful things about language: don't say ethnography, say case study; don't say re-appropriate or negotiate, say impact or effect. Then I also learn that just about everything about my project will turn most people off to speaking with me and that I will have to learn how to ask without asking. Policy and race are big issues at the school, but they will shut people down. Sports on the other hand will get people going a mile a minute. After 45 minutes of good advice peppered with sardonic humor, he mentions that he always had a slight crush on the lovely Greek woman behind the counter and commences to engage her in innocent conversation. I leave wondering where methodology intersects with my practice, this idea I have of how research is like getting into trouble, and whether trouble will actually play out in the field or only when I'm sitting at my desk.

(Field Notes, Late Spring 2008)

2

OHIO MAGNET SCHOOL BEFORE AND AFTER *BROWN*

Sharing what I learned about Ohio Magnet School (OMS) and experiencing the almost unavoidable reinscription of urban stereotypes made clear that there was no way out of the entanglement of discourse, history, and representation. The next section identifies some of the larger discursive frameworks circulating within social science research that I argue fix and contain urban student identity. The goal here is to begin a process of deconstructing the frameworks of disadvantage, deprivation, and risk that hold sway so that the analysis can work against the tendencies for their unacknowledged sedimentation. I believe that disrupting the damaging discourses of urban identity is imperative in attempting to do ethical work with these students. To start from the very place that reinscribes stereotypes about their educational engagement further contributes to their marginalization.

The Politics of Who's at Risk

OMS was recognized in 2007 by the National Center for Urban School Transformation for its ability to transform the urban school setting into one "where all students achieve academic proficiency, evidence a love of learning, and graduate well prepared to succeed in post-secondary education, the workplace, and their communities." The idea of transformation brought to mind what Fine (1995) called "the politics of who's at risk." What and who is in need of transforming and how is transformation thought about in urban schools? As Fine states:

> The language of "risk" is upon us, piercing daily consciousness, educational practices, and bureaucratic policy-making. Scholars, practitioners, and activists have been quick to name, identify, and ossify those who

> presumably suffer at the mercy of "risk factors." It satisfies both the desire to isolate these people, by the Right, and to display them, by the Left.
>
> *(p. 77)*

This idea of transformation works in tandem with historical images and sedimented cultural representations to make possible particular conceptualizations of urban schools and students, and suppress others. For OMS to be recognized as an example of the excellence possible in urban education, it requires a dominant image of urban schooling where students fail academically and socially. These images are in ready supply. The idea of transformation capitalizes on and requires urban students to be represented as unsuccessful, at risk, and struggling with cultural competencies. This conceptualization of urban education cannot function without its at-risk urban Other. It both contains and displays them. It evades the historical backdrop of racialized schooling practices that have created the conditions for what is now referred to as "urban education."

Urban education gives meaning to race and frames itself particularly as a democratic project concerned with equity and access. Though the unspecified term "urban" is most often used, race functions in meaningful ways within and through the bodies of its students. Urban students, their raced and classed bodies, and what they signify become useful in showcasing education's transformative effects on "the disadvantaged." It capitalizes on and solidifies historic and racialized narratives of the always failing, culturally deprived student of color, and for OMS that is the Black student, and excludes the history of Black education in the US, the failures of integration, and the implications of these failures for urban schools today.

How does the exploitation of these students mask the racism of the past and forestall the possibility for real social change? How might urban student identity and subjectivity then be reconceived? How might urban education as a democratic project function without its ahistoric, agent-less, disadvantaged Other? How can we use the wreckage of the past to see the possibilities of an urban education that recognizes its failures within the context of racism? How might the tensions between access and excellence be rethought and reconceived? These are the problematics of this study as I set out to work within and against notions of urban identity. How did we get here and how might we find a different starting place for thinking about urban students, one that takes seriously students' material experiences of inequality without wresting their own agency from their grasp?

Undoing the Urban Child as Other

Concepts and theories of 'child saving,' 'cultural deprivation,' 'culture of poverty,' and 'tangle of pathology' will be interrogated here as discourses generated by social science research that produce the iterative manifestations of urban student identity. In a sense, these discourses circuitously feed off one another, simultaneously satisfying the conditions for the continual representation of the urban other as defined within their constraints, fixing the limits of representation, and therefore solidifying their explanatory power. Social science research provides the context for thinking about how to do ethical research in urban schools that is held accountable for how it others its subjects.

Moving forward, I first present a brief historical summary of racial migration in and out of urban centers and the forces that promoted these migrations and led to the reconceptualization of urban identity. Next, I trace the discourses mentioned above to further consider the conditions of possibility for raced and classed articulations of urban students in research. Following this review, I will use Yon's notion of 'elusive culture' (1999) as a way to fluidly reframe the lived experiences of students so that the materialities of their lives matter, but they are not robbed of their agency to live differently.

Toward a History of Racial Migration, Representation, and Urban Educational Identity

In the latter half of the nineteenth century, European immigration and industrialization contributed to the expansion and growth of urban cities. The surge in population in urban centers without infrastructure created conditions for overcrowding, inadequate sanitation and human services, and the spread of disease. Urban schooling was largely concerned with the assimilation and control of a growing European ethnic population to reduce the delinquency, poverty, and crime that seemed inherent to city life (Spring, 2005/1986, pp. 206–207).

Over the course of the early twentieth century, European ethnic groups slowly became homogenized and accepted into dominant white society (Roediger, 2002). At the same time, Blacks were migrating to the industrial north for jobs and settling in urban areas and cities. Giddings (1996/1984) notes that between 1915 and 1920 approximately 500,000 Black men and women transplanted families to fill the demand for workers in industry and domestic service in the north (p. 141).

Beginning as early as the 1930s, government home ownership programs channeled loan funding toward whites, including newly homogenized white ethnics, and away from communities of color. This gap in resources gave whites capital to move out of the cities and into predominantly white enclaves. It depleted resources needed to improve urban housing and economies, and left Black Americans with limited opportunities for community investment and improvement. As a result of this white flight, urban areas became predominantly Black and under-resourced. Federal highway programs destroyed urban housing to connect the suburbs, and urban renewal and gentrification initiatives displaced people of color into further segregated and isolated pockets (Lipsitz, 1998). This manifestation of racially impacted social and economic forces produced the conditions through which urban centers came to be seen and experienced as predominantly Black and poor.

From Childsaving Social Policy to Culture as Pathology

Swadener (1995) argued that US "childsaving" social policy has been heavily connected with urban growth and development, with roots as far back as the late 1700s. Early on childsaving identified particular groups of white European ethnic children (i.e., children with handicaps and diseases, orphans, indigents, delinquents, the abused and neglected) as requiring social concern and responsibility. Her analysis located discourses of risk and disadvantage across disciplines of medicine, the social sciences, education, public policy, economics, and demography. Discourses of disadvantage as perpetuated in these disciplines were a part of urban identity construction and childsaving throughout history (pp. 17–28).

Laosa (as cited in Swadener, 1995), argued that the identification of children along lines of race as 'at risk' was a recent phenomenon. This shift in discourse was connected in part to the transformation of urban centers from "white to black" that was produced through Black migration and white flight. With this demographic shift, childsaving discourses of disadvantage also shifted reference from the white child to the Black child. In and through these shifts, childsaving discourses came to be articulations of concern for urban, Black youth, constructing new limits of representation and processes of othering.

Social science research in education engaged this articulation, promotion, and perpetuation of concerns for the urban Black child. Deficit discourses of cultural deprivation, cultural poverty, and risk were put in direct conversation with understandings of educational achievement, interjecting a particular formation of an urban educational identity into the collective American lexicon that bound together underachievement with Black culture.

Recalling *Brown v. Board of Education* (1954), plaintiffs built a portion of the case on social science research into the effects of state-imposed racial segregation on Black children. The evidence took a two-pronged approach arguing: 1) against scientific racism, making the case that there were no scientific rationales for the classification of children by race; and 2) that Black children had been harmed by poverty, racism, and the absence of interracial contact (Ravitch, 1983, p. 126). While the arguments made were instrumental in bringing about the *Brown* decision, the latter half of the argument set the stage for urban education research and its focus on the cultural deprivation of Black children.

Cultural deprivation research argued that poverty and racial prejudice impaired the ability to learn, and that schools were ineffective in adapting methods to the needs of these students. Social scientists argued the root problem to be the home environments that did not transmit the cultural knowledge necessary for school success (Ravitch, 1983, p. 152). One of the most influential educational studies was Coleman's (1966) report, *Equality of Educational Opportunity*, also referred to as "The Coleman Report." The major findings of the report asserted that: 1) most students attended schools where the majority of pupils were of the same race; 2) white schools did have advantages in physical resources, but differences were less than anticipated; 3) the academic achievement of Black students was typically anywhere from 1–5 years behind whites depending on the year in school; 4) achievement was related to a student's family background rather than school quality; and 5) next to family background, the social composition of the school and the student's sense of control over the environment were important factors in success (Ravitch, 1983, pp. 168–169). Through these findings, lagging achievement in Black schools came to be equated with racial isolation, family background, and social composition.

The Coleman report and the evidence presented in *Brown* further solidified discursively the stigmatization of Black schools, families, and culture. Though reports like Coleman's fueled the integration movement, the coupling of integration and the notion that achievement was more connected to family background than school quality "actually heightened the stigma attached to schools attended by minority pupils" and affirmed that "minority neighborhoods were inferior no matter what their resources or programs" (Ravitch, 1983, p. 173). Racial isolation became identified as the structural problematic that bred cultural deprivation. The power/knowledge effects of these findings articulated *underachievement* with Blackness and *achievement* to whiteness. Underachievement became a mark of the educational other. It simultaneously uncoupled student achievement from institutional advantage and school quality.

Forming a response to the cultural deprivation model, anthropologist Oscar Lewis constructed the culture of poverty model as "a counterdiscourse to notions of familial instability and disorganization," like those notions presented in cultural deprivation theories, "as well as an alternative to biological notions of race and poverty" (Gonzalez, 2004, p. 20). The culture of poverty was assigned a series of traits engendered by the poor that came to be justifications for the academic failure of poor children. Gonzalez argued that "(t)he idea that poor students were shaped by a culture of poverty that was considered to be antithetical to the deferred gratification inherent in school achievement was in large part responsible for the development of cultural deficit models of schooling" (p. 20). Through these lines of logic, the cultures of poor and minority students also came to be targeted as the cause of their own educational failure. Rather than serving as a discursive intervention, discourses of cultural deprivation retraced the limits of urban identity, re-satisfied its conditions, and re-substantiated the necessity of the urban other in education.

Another attempt at intervention that was productive of and produced by these discourses was an oft-cited piece of research on the culture of poverty, *The Negro Family: The Case for National Action* (United States Department of Labor, 1965). Published by the Office of Policy Planning and Research at the

US Department of Labor, it is also referred to as the "Moynihan Report." Spearheaded by then Senator Daniel Patrick Moynihan to draw national attention to the War on Poverty, this report argued, "the fundamental source of the weakness of the Negro community" and "of the fabric of Negro society is the deterioration of the Negro family" (p. 5). Defined by a matriarchal family structure, it was attributed with the breakdown of urban centers, the dissolution of marriages, the rate of illegitimate births, increased welfare dependency, and an entire "tangle of pathology" blamed for the failure of its youth. The report drew a great deal of fire from the Black community, yet no one was more surprised than Moynihan who felt he made a painstaking attempt to be racially sensitive and objective (Giddings, 1996/1984, pp. 327–328).

Historically tracing the discourses and conditions that made possible a particular way of seeing urban educational identity establishes a context for the current representations of urban students and schools. Urban identity formation is contingent upon historic, racial, economic, and social forces that have created the context, or grid of knowledge, fomenting the production of urban as synonymous with Black, poor, and culturally disadvantaged. *Brown* brought race to the forefront of educational research and US consciousness in new ways, and social science research attempted to understand urban identity, but with unfortunate consequences. As demonstrated here, despite its best intentions to be otherwise, social research and policy have accumulated their own "troubled legacy" of blaming Black culture for inequality.

In the current moment, the words "urban" and "high poverty," signifiers for OMS, also appear to stand in for race. Delineating OMS as an urban school both identifies it innocuously as a school with specific issues related to its city location, and it simultaneously capitalizes on the hidden discourse of race so tightly tied to historical urban representations. At the same time, the term "culture" has worked at the interstices of race and poverty, and slowly come to stand in for these. It has permitted the production of referents like urban, inner city, disadvantaged, underprivileged, and at risk, which elide race into culture and facilitate tacit avoidance of race-specific or racialized issues.

The Problem of Culture

The problem of culture, according to Yon (1999), is that it is haunted by its own ghost. In spite of the crisis of representation that occurred within the social sciences that shattered a reliance on the timelessness and given-ness of societies and individuals, 'culture' continues to stand in for fixed identities, knowable properties, and a distinct way of being and seeing that belongs to a particular group of people, bound somehow by lived experience. Yon (2000) posited the concept of 'elusive culture' as a way to divest oneself from the dominant trope of culture to see it more significantly as an on-going process that has the capacity to exceed and complicate what is considered to be "given" and "known" (pp. 4–5). He situates race as a product of discourse fluidly constructed through relations of knowledge and power that are both historically and structurally (macro), and locally and specifically (micro), contingent. This gives way to the possibility to see race as a relational experience as opposed to a phenotypically driven and totalizing phenomenon (p. 131).

Elusive culture for Yon (1999) is a question of becoming and not just being. This moves the direction of analysis toward thinking about not only how identity is formed, but also how students are subjects in the making, remaking, and resisting of identity. Culture then is revised as both a product and a process, discursively situated within the grid of power and knowledge, but permeable to the complicated ways students live their lives. Yon's conception of race and culture as elusive and fluid lends itself well to thinking about how students are agents in refashioning urban educational identity on their own terms.

The idea of elusivity provides a different approach to the problem of culture, which pushes this study to be attentive to materialities of structural inequality experienced by students in urban schools while recognizing the contingencies, relationality, and unboundedness of their lived experience. By seeing students as elusive subjects, I recognize that they are not fully knowable, will resist my grasp, and exceed my expectations for what it means to be an urban student in a high-achieving, high-poverty school.

A unique piece of OMS history often forgotten is the historical and racial context within which OMS was created and how its identity has been shaped over the years by the racial politics of education in Columbus, Ohio. Before it was an urban success story, it was a predominantly white alternative school for advanced students seeking an independent education. What precipitated this change in the student body and its public identity? This next section sketches the impact of the *Brown* decision on Columbus City Schools (CCS) to frame the historical position within which OMS now sits as an *urban* school.

A Troubled Legacy

The *Brown v. Board of Education* (1954) decision sits at the nexus of law, research, and educational policy and their collaborative efforts to redefine educational goals toward equality. According to Bell (1995), the genesis of *Brown* can be traced back to court cases as early as the mid-nineteenth century that brought numerous suits against segregated schooling (p. 6). Beginning in the 1930s, the National Association for the Advancement of Colored People (NAACP) developed a coordinated legal campaign strategy against segregation, using the courts as a form of redress to challenge the constitutionality of *separate but equal*. In 1953 and 1954, they spearheaded a series of direct challenges to the constitutionality of state-enforced segregation in K-12 education. Public schooling was chosen as the battleground, because it "presented a far more compelling symbol of the evils of segregation and a far more vulnerable target than segregated railroad cars, restaurants, restrooms" (Bell, 1995, p. 6). A group of cases from Kansas, South Carolina, Delaware, Virginia, and the District of Columbia, known collectively as *Brown v. Board of Education* (1954), challenged the *Plessey v. Ferguson* (1896) decision that *separate but equal* was indeed legal and just.

A portion of the plaintiffs' case was built on social science research into the effects of state-imposed racial segregation on Black children. The evidence took a double pronged approach arguing: 1) against scientific racism, making the case that there were no scientific rationales for the classification of children by race; and 2) that Black children and their already presumed cultural deficits had been further exacerbated by poverty, racism, and the absence of interracial contact (Ravitch, 1983, p. 126). The plaintiffs also made a color-blind argument that the Fourteenth Amendment precluded state action based on race and color. This combination of argumentation successfully achieved a Supreme Court ruling declaring state-imposed racial segregation in public schools unconstitutional. The *Brown* decision represented not only the long sought recognition that American practices of segregation were in opposition to its egalitarian ideals, but it also represented a potential means to achieving substantive equality (Ravitch, 1983, pp. 124–132). However, as critical race theorists and historians have demonstrated, the court ruling was in many ways ineffective in ending segregated schooling.

While the arguments made were instrumental in bringing about the *Brown* decision, both the color-blind argument and the discourse of Black inferiority perpetuated the definition of Black students as inferior, at risk, and disadvantaged, and negated the need to address the underlying systemic pathologies of racism and white supremacy both inside and outside of the school system (Ladson-Billings, 2004). Anderson (2004) argued that "contemporary rationales for educational inequality are linked to a legacy of blaming racial subordination on African American personality traits and cultural norms" (p. 359) and that this "victim blaming" has fostered assumptions of a culture of anti-intellectualism and deprivation that is held primarily responsible for achievement gaps between Blacks, and other students of color, and whites in student performance (p. 362). As current research has demonstrated, teacher thinking and practices continue to be informed by deficit beliefs about urban students, their families, and their cultures (Garcia and Guerra, 2004; Milner IV, 2008).

Anderson (2006) referred to *Brown* as a "troubled legacy" holding both a "time honored place in America's longstanding pursuit for formal equality under the law and its unfulfilled promises of substantive equality in American public education" (p. 16). Ladson-Billings (2004) noted its "mythic quality" and our tendency to see it as an example of a steady march toward racial progress "that is coupled with a view of America as a nation endowed with inherent 'goodness' and exceptionality" (p. 3). As Bell (1980) made clear, though *Brown* has a legacy that cannot be forgotten, "most black children attend public schools that are both racially isolated and inferior. Demographic patterns, white flight, and the inability of the courts to effect the necessary degree of social reform render further progress in implementing *Brown* almost impossible" (p. 518). Orfield and Lee's (2004) work on patterns of resegregation confirms Bell's assertion; data collected during the years of their study, 1991 through 2001, showed that segregated schooling had increased rather than decreased 20 years after the landmark legislation (p. 2). Ohio exhibited climbing resegregation rates during this 10-year period, and as a result was ranked as the 14th most segregated state for Black students in 2001 (p. 27). The proportion of Black students attending intensely segregated minority schools has more than doubled between 1991 and 2005 in the state of Ohio (Orfield and Lee, 2007).

OMS and CCS have their own rich histories that must be accounted for to understand how OMS functions as a successful urban high school. By focusing on the local historical context of Black education in Columbus before and after *Brown*, a different history is presented for thinking about the education of Black children in urban schools (and all students from disadvantaged backgrounds), one that emphasizes the legacy of academic success in the Black community before integration.

Black public education in Columbus, Ohio before *Brown* was relatively successful before the Supreme Court ruled in favor of *Brown v. Board of Education*. In *Getting Around Brown: Desegregation, Development and the Columbus Public Schools* (1998), Jacobs provided a historical account of the viable social, political, and economic community that thrived in Columbus before attempts at integration began. Black public schooling found ways to thrive in spite of segregation. As Columbus manipulated attendance boundaries and unofficially produced race-based school districts, African Americans created all Black schools that garnered a highly qualified staff. They found ways to gain representation on the school board and advocate for their community. Local schools that today have poor reputations then embodied the promise and possibility of (segregated) education (Jacobs, pp. 10–19).

In the wake of *Brown* and the Civil Rights movement, President Lyndon Johnson gathered momentum to persuade the congress to pass, after more than 100 years of debate, the Elementary and Secondary Education Act of 1965 (ESEA), which sought to remedy inequality through financing and other legislative measure to support education. With desegregation, it became more readily apparent to the government and white society that there were wide disparities in opportunity, resources, and achievement between Black and white children, suburban, rural, and urban children, and across class differences. Simultaneously, desegregation also brought about concerns from white parents about the lowering of educational standards as integration proceeded (Ravitch, 1983, pp. 148–149).

Jacobs (1998) chronicles the middle-class abandonment of the CCS District, even after the 1978 *Penick v. Columbus Board of Education* decision attempted to bring an end to uneven desegregation practices of gerrymandering and redlining that Columbus realtors and developers used somewhat successfully to "get around Brown." With *Penick I* (1977), Ohio Supreme Court Justice Robert Duncan ruled that the CCS District was guilty of maintaining systematically and intentionally a dual district that was racially segregated and required it to desegregate. This was followed in 1978 by *Penick II*, in which Duncan again ruled in favor of the plaintiffs, this time requiring a system-wide plan to desegregate every school in the district. Consequentially, as Columbus instituted integration, white families fled to the growing suburbs.

It was in the eye of this storm that OMS was created as one of the first lottery-based magnet schools in the district designed to attract and/or keep (white and middle-class) families. As explained to me during an interview with a senior teacher who had been with the school since 1982, OMS began in 1978 as a predominantly white alternative half-day program that quickly acquired local and national recognition, which allowed it to secure full-day operations in 1980. Though it was successful in attracting an academically driven set of predominantly white parents and students, alternative schools like it were not enough to stem the tide of outmigration. As seen in Figure 2.1,[1] the demographic constituency of the district slowly shifted from predominantly white to majority African American.

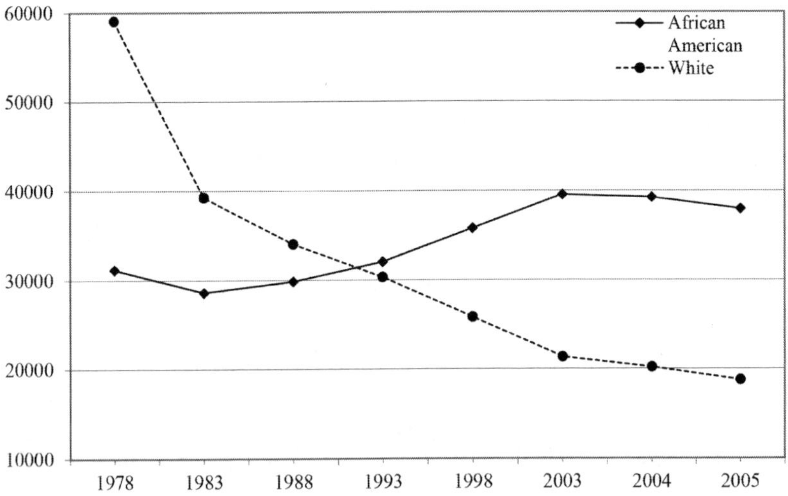

FIGURE 2.1 After 1978, the racial distribution of students in the district began to shift. Prior to the Penick decisions, Columbus City Schools had been predominantly white. When the Supreme Court required the desegregation of every school in the district, white families began to leave the school system for private schools and the suburbs. As a result, by the early 1990s, the district achieved racial parity and then quickly transitioned to a predominantly Black school system.

In 1985 Justice Robert Duncan released Columbus City Schools from court-ordered desegregation. Shortly thereafter, the school board pursued a plan to restructure school assignment patterns, add more alternative schools, and reduce bussing. During these years, Columbus schools created a policy of racial balancing for the lottery schools, which was later abandoned as unnecessary (Jacobs, 1998, pp. 157–161). OMS continued to reflect the demographic trends of white outmigration in the district, developing into a predominantly Black high school by the mid-1990s (see Figure 2.2).

This account of CCS demonstrates how court cases like *Brown v. Board of Education* (1954) had specific implications for formulating education's response to race, its democratic intention to provide access, and the perceived competing tension with preserving excellence. In spite of Supreme Court rulings like *Brown* and *Penick*, segregation was unofficially maintained. The legacy of segregated schooling legislation is encapsulated by the paradox of the discernible gains from civil rights and the subtle and insidious reformulation of racism and oppression that maintains inequality and disadvantage in public schooling and society. To understand OMS, we must grasp its location within this history.

After *Brown*, the school district took symbolic measures toward integration while the city continued housing and employment practices that perpetuated segregation. It was a pattern that maintained the unequal conditions and structural inequalities that plague its urban schools and communities today. Yet this history is forgotten, and the implications of race and resistances to *Brown* recede into the background. Historically, Black education in Columbus emphasized *success*,

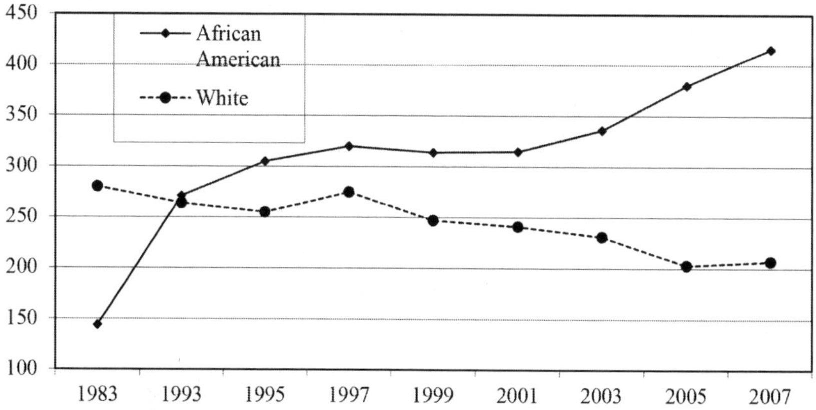

FIGURE 2.2 OMS began as a predominantly white alternative program. However, the program was unable to stem the tide of white outmigration affecting the district. Following a trend similar to Columbus Public Schools, OMS developed into a predominantly Black high school by the mid 1990s and continued to have increasing enrollments for Black students and decreasing enrollments for white students.

excellence, and *achievement* and knowing this history shows how these characteristics are ever-present in urban public education, though they are absent in current mainstream talk about urban schools. What does it mean to think about the future of urban education today by acknowledging this legacy? I believe urban schools and students can be seen differently if the starting point is with traditions of success rather than assumptions of intrinsic failure. With this history in mind, the next section provides a descriptive snapshot of OMS.

A Snapshot of Ohio Magnet School

OMS has a 35-year history as a college preparatory public school deeply invested in academic achievement and is nationally recognized as a "breakthrough school," "urban school of promise," and school of "excellence."[2] While its accolades are too numerous to list, the most impressive include being recognized in 2015 by Newsweek as one of the Top 25 Transformative High Schools in the US.

Located in a low-income neighborhood on the east side of the city, the racial and socioeconomic demographics of the student body closely mimic the demographics of other schools in its district—at the time of the study, 65.5 percent of the student body was African American, 27.7 percent white, 3 percent Asian or Pacific Islander, and 2.5 percent Latino. Fifty-five percent of all students were eligible to receive free or reduced lunch. However, its high rate of academic achievement set it apart—OMS maintains an average graduation rate of 99 percent, compared to the district average of 73 percent, and an average college attendance rate of 96 percent, including entrance to ivy league institutions. According to its website, recent graduates have earned over $8 million in scholarships. Students from all over CCS enter a lottery each year for the opportunity to enroll. At the time of the study, OMS accepted approximately 150 students to the 9th grade from over 1,000 applicants.

This school was provided with the same limited infrastructural and curricular resources as other schools, or as parents and teachers would argue, it was given far fewer resources with which to work. Yet it offered an exclusively college preparatory curriculum that included Advanced Placement (AP), the only International Baccalaureate (IB) program in the district, and it was well known for its humanities-based curriculum that served as a model for other schools. It fostered an academically based culture characterized by high expectations and respect, a rigorous curriculum, and intrinsically motivated teachers, students, and parents. The school did not have an interscholastic sports program, which participants perceived also contributed to the culture of success. Each student was expected to graduate with a certificate of college preparation. They were required to enroll in a math, science, social studies, and foreign language course each year, and complete an internship during their last three years of high school. Parents and staff stated that the environment made students feel "called to excellence" and "empowered . . . like they have a stake in their success."

OMS students were also ascribed an unmistakable quality that set them apart, but this quality was often difficult for people to describe. According to the guidance counselor Mrs. Cowan, "Everybody says that OMS students just look a certain way . . . We know that there are certain things, a certain style that it brings, and it brings maturity." The other guidance counselor, Mrs. Altman agreed, "There's that certain mindset, that certain worldliness that they get here."

The teachers and administration were passionate, enthusiastic, and hard working. "They're all working over their contractual limits," the Principal told me during an interview, and "they don't complain." When hiring new teachers, OMS was sure to discuss with applicants the culture of high expectations that exist for staff, and, as a result, some applicants made decisions to take positions at other schools. The teachers spoke on several occasions about the importance of working collaboratively outside of school to prepare assignments and field trips because, as the freshman humanities teacher, Mrs. Scott, explained, "Our students just deserve that the curriculum be taught the way it is supposed to." According to the Ohio Department of Education, in 2008, 79 percent of the teachers held at least a master's degree, and several of the teachers and the Principal either held doctorates or pursued doctoral studies.

But as Mr. Hart, a social studies teacher, explained, there is more to it than just working hard:

> There were a handful of teachers here, and what I thought was interesting, all the teachers I saw have 25 to 30 years of experience and they were here on sort of their day off, a snow day, and I just thought that . . . there's not a sense of complacency. People that have 25 years experience and they're coming in because they know they have to get prepared and they have a lot of work to do . . . *How do you recreate a school like this? How do you . . . recreate who comes in on a snow day? What if you start a school with no teachers that come in on a snow day?*

The PTA was often recognized for its strength and ability to shore up this under-resourced school, and its visibility inside and outside of the building. They worked hard to write and win grants to increase their budget, which allowed them to provided back-up funds for the library, theater, the arts, chorus, and other extra programs, and they purchased supplies and provided labor for outdoor improvements. They provided breakfast for staff each month and celebrated students that passed the Ohio Graduation Test with a cupcake. They had also purchased textbooks in the past for entire classes and for individual students who were unable to purchase their own summer reading materials.

The PTA also assumed a political identity in the community. A parent new to the PTA commented on the uncharacteristic involvement:

> I have never seen a PTA such as is here. I cannot believe it. I mean sometimes it's like whoa! But very politically oriented, and they actually make

> changes in the school. I mean, they'll go to the school board . . . I've participated in other PTAs but when I came here I was like WOW, they're gonna burn the building in a minute.

This snapshot provides a favorable overview of OMS, the typical victory narrative operationalized when stories are told about this truly successful school. It is based on a well-deserved reputation that attracts journalists and inspires awards and accolades, but it also elides the complexities of educational policy in practice and the material experiences of urban students and families as they negotiate race, class, and identity. It's an ahistorical feel-good story that cuts it away from the social contingencies, discourses, and power relations that sustain it. Though at first glance it appears to elevate representations of urban students, the narrative is sustained by a sense of exceptionalism that expects urban students to always fail rather than succeed. This romantic view of urban students effectively freezes and fixes them within the stagnant discourses of disadvantage and risk. I am writing both within and against this story.

The next chapter takes an in-depth look at how the culture of high expectations was sustained in spite of the heavy hand of educational policy. I argue that by offering only college preparatory courses within a culture of achievement, OMS appeared to be re-appropriating No Child Left Behind policies in ways that undid some of the constraining effects of accountability, like "teaching to the test." OMS redefined accountability on its own terms through the higher standards of an all-inclusive college prep curriculum that incorporated AP and IB programs. And students rose to the challenge.

Notes

1 I compiled the data for Figures 2.1 and 2.2 based on published enrollment tables available through the Ohio Department of Education. The 1983 data on Figure 2.2 were estimated from a high school yearbook to establish early enrollment by race, as no data existed prior to 1993.

2 References for news, magazine, and other media will not be provided in order to protect the identities of the school and participants.

References

Anderson, J. D. (2004). Crosses to bear and promises to keep: The jubilee anniversary of *Brown v. Board of Education*. *Urban Education*, *39*(4), 359–373.

Anderson, J. D. (2006). A tale of two Browns: Constitutional equality and unequal education. *Yearbook—National Society for the Study of Education*, *105*(2), 14–35.

Bell, D. A. (1980). *Brown v Board of Education* and the interest convergence dilemma. *Harvard Educational Review*, *93*, 518–533.

Bell, D. A. (1995). Serving two masters: Integration ideals and client interests in school desegregation litigation. In K. Crenchshaw, N. Gotanda, G. Peller, and K. Thomas (Eds.), *Critical Race Theory: The Key Writings That Formed the Movement* (pp. 5–19). New York: New Press.

Brown v. Board of Education of Topeka, 347 U.S. 483. (1954).

Coleman, J. S. (1966). *Equality of Educational Opportunity*. Washington, DC: National Center for Educational Statistics.

Fine, M. (1995). The politics of who's at risk. In B. Blue Swadener and S. Lubeck (Eds.), *Children and Families at Promise: Deconstructing the Discourse of Risk* (pp. 76–94). Albany, NY: State University of New York Press.

Garcia, S. B., and Guerra, P. L. (2004). Deconstructing deficit thinking: Working with educators to create more equitable learning environments. *Educatiuon and Urban Society, 36*(2), 150–168.

Giddings, P. (1996/1984). *When and Where I Enter: The Impact of Black Women on Race and Sex in America*. New York, NY: William Morrow and Company.

Gonzalez, N. (2004). Disciplining the discipline: Anthropology and the pursuit of quality education. *Educational Researcher, 33*(5), 17–25.

Jacobs, G. (1998). *Getting around Brown: Desegregation, Development, and the Columbus Public Schools*. Columbus, OH: Ohio State University Press.

Ladson-Billings, G. (2004). Landing on the wrong note: The price we paid for *Brown*. *Educational Researcher, 33*(7), 3–13.

Lipsitz, G. (1998). *The Possessive Investment in Whiteness: How White People Profit from Identity Politics*. Philadelphia, PA: Temple University Press.

Milner, R. (2008). Disrupting deficit notions of difference: Counter-narratives of teachers and community in urban education. *Teacher and Teacher Education, 24*(6), 1573–1598.

No Child Left Behind Act, 20 U.S.C. § 6301, (2001).

Orfield, G. and Lee, C. (2004). *Brown at 50: King's Dream or Plessy's Nightmare?* Cambridge, MA: The Civil Rights Project at Harvard University.

Orfield, G. and Lee, C. (2007). *Historic Reversals, Accelerating Resegregation, and the Need for New Integration Strategies*. Los Angeles, CA: UCLA, Civil Rights Project.

Penick v. Columbus Board of Education, 429 F Supp. 229. (1977).

Penick v. Columbus, Board of Education, 583 F. 2d 787. (1978).

Plessy v. Ferguson, 163 U.S. 537. (1896).

Ravitch, D. (1983). *The Troubled Crusade: American Education 1945–1980*. New York: Basic Books.

Roediger, D. (2002). Whiteness and ethnicity in the history of white ethnics in the United States. In O. Essed and D. T. Goldbert (Eds.), *Race Critical Theories: Text and Context* (pp. 325–343). Malden, MA: Blackwell Publishers.

Spring, J. (2005/1986). *The American School 1642–2004* (6th ed.). New York: McGraw Hill.

Swadener, B. (1995). Children and families "at promise": Deconstructing the discourse of risk. In B. Swadener and S. Lubeck (Eds.), *Children and Families "At Promise": Deconstructing the Discourse of Risk* (pp. 17–49). Albany, NY: State University of New York Press.

United States Department of Labor. (1965). *The Negro Family: The Case for National Action*. Washington, DC: Author.

Yon, D. (1999). Pedagogy and the problem of "difference": On reading community in the darker side of black. *International Journal of Qualitative Studies in Education, 12*(6), 623–641.

Yon, D. (2000). *Elusive Culture: Schooling, Race, and Identity in Global Times*. Albany, NY: State University of New York Press.

"SEE WHAT WE DON'T HAVE"

The Myth of the Boutique School

Most of the classrooms at OMS have rows of tightly packed chairs, old computers, and just barely enough space at the front of the room for a teacher's desk and a place to stand. White boards were installed during winter break, and this was the extent of updating that I saw while conducting research.

Dented gray lockers line the first and second floor hallways. The auditorium is too small to hold the entire school. The gym floors and bleachers are original, but considering that there are no sports at this school, it is safe to assume that the gym is a last priority. The cafeteria is small, with standard folding tables. The lunchroom fills to capacity during each of the three lunch periods, and excess students overflow into the gym in the winter and the backyard and blacktop courts during warmer weather, playing basketball or football. Ten or so students typically brave the cold and sit at picnic tables in the courtyard, while a few others stand in the back hallways next to an empty Pepsi machine and a snack machine that is partially filled.

The Principal, Dr. Davis, explained prior to coming to the school in 2008, even she had the perception, "that OMS had everything, everything you could imagine was here at OMS. And it just wasn't so." She talked about her struggle to improve the facility for teachers and students, often at her own expense. Dr. Davis' office lacked adequate furniture to accommodate her tall frame. She worked on a computer at a short wooden desk, a collapsible table full of papers served as a credenza, and a few mismatched wooden chairs sat up against the wall for guests.

It was important to her that the school looked nice for the students and staff, "Something that small makes a difference, but it says to me that we care enough; even though we may not have a lot of nice things we're going to make it look nice." When she arrived, she asked the janitors to re-arrange the desks so that each room had desks that matched in color. She went to the district warehouse to get 200 more desks, and when she refused to take the desks that did not match, warehouse staff complained to her boss that she had "an attitude." She explained:

> *I said, "why should we get the trash. I'm working with trash now and trying to clean it up. I'm sitting in my office with two tables" . . . I'm thinking, "I don't have to have the best of the best here as long as the students and teachers have what they need, then I'll wait. But right now it's important for the teachers to get what they need."*

Parents were also shocked at the facilities when they made their first visits to OMS. The parent of a new freshman explained:

> *The facility is terrible. It's unbelievable to me. They have chemistry labs with no chemicals. They can't really perform experiments. They can't weigh things, they have these ancient scales. They don't have any real balances. Pieces of ceiling fall down all the time. The heating and air conditioner are nonexistent . . . You see mice running around the auditorium when we're in there . . . There are kids who faint in the heat when school first starts. It's unbelievably hot in that building. The auditorium is pathetic.*

Parents, teachers, and administrators were also aware of the lack of technology at the school. One parent told me in an agitated voice, "Our dag gone clocks aren't even set." Dr. Davis acquired 30 outdated computers that another school was discarding to construct the first full-service computer lab OMS had ever had.

She discussed taking a visiting school board member on a tour of the school to "see what we don't have." "I'm trying to get the whole building wireless," she tells me.

> *Where are the smart boards, where are computers, where are the laptops? . . . because I want to make sure they have everything that the kids at (her previous school) have. Because I made sure they had the top everything. They might not have utilized it as much as the kids here, but they have it accessible to them.*

Her previous high school was a low-achieving program with a very successful athletic department.

OMS' extracurricular activities, like chorale and theatre, were underfunded. The library was lacking resources. The librarian described the difficulty filling in the deficits in her collection for research projects and extended essays: "the only budget you get basically is pleading with the principal to cough up something . . . The minute you get into a school like this that needs resources that are at a higher level, you're looking at college level type text books and reference that are costing $75 to start." The PTA was her best source for funds; small and private grants, she said, were difficult due to the approval process one has to go through with the district. Her explanation of how schools get resources is telling of the mixed effects NCLB has on high-performing urban schools:

> *Well, the equity is I guess if you score low, you get all the prizes. You don't need help, apparently you're doing well. That's basically how the trickle down process*

> *works in the district. And since we were high performing, we're bottom on the list for little perks.*

Teachers and parents perceived that the lottery created a situation in which staff at other schools harbored resentment toward those at OMS, and that this contributed to their access to resources. As Mr. Fisher explained, "But there have been efforts, real or imagined, by people outside the school . . . I've heard people in the past say they want to break us . . . there are people who resent OMS. They think we get too much." Mr. Westfall, one of the IB teachers, saw a connection between the success of their students and the assumptions people made that the school gets preferential treatment, "(We're) getting more funding. (We're) getting the best people. (We're) circumventing the lottery to get in that place. This is not fair."

It's apparent once you cross the threshold of OMS that success is not guaranteed by excellent resources and infrastructure, and this excellence is not the result of privilege, advantage, or special treatment.

3

"STATE STANDARDS ARE THE MINIMUM OF WHAT WE DO"

The (Constraining) Effects of No Child Left Behind (NCLB)

A long-sought intention of NCLB was to raise the overall achievement of all students and close the achievement gap between minority and high-poverty students and their white, affluent counterparts. However, analysis of the legislation and evidence from early implementation led researchers to argue that the act would ultimately fail itself, fail children, and fail society (Fusarelli, 2004).

Viewed as "intrusive and non-negotiable" (Gay, 2007), NCLB created unintended negative consequences for public schools that policymakers ignored. Opponents argued that testing culture promoted a narrowed curriculum, focused on low-level skills and high-stakes test training, replacing rich critical inquiry and maximum potential with rote memorization and minimum expectations governed by a testing regime that undermined teachers, students, and schools. High-stakes testing bound to public accountability provided strong incentives for schools to exclude or ignore low-performing students and led to an increase, rather than a decrease, in the drop out rate. A diversity penalty haunted schools that served the most disadvantaged students with the threat of lost funding or even closure if they failed to improve, and this encouraged schools to push out, keep out, or drop out low-scoring students. Some of the neediest students, like English language learners and special needs students, were held to inappropriate standards and expectations, and suffered from a lack of appropriate support to make academic progress, also leading to increased levels of drop out. Public shaming, intimidation, and punishment experienced through the labelling of failing schools and the resulting reduction in funding and incentives to these needy programs not only demoralized teachers themselves but also reduced the ability of schools and districts to attract and retain high-quality educators, another intended goal of the bill (Darling-Hammond, 2007; Gay, 2007; Hursh, 2007).

This chapter looks at how Ohio Magnet School (OMS) avoided this fate. It successfully negotiated a strict set of policies and undermined the constraining effects in ways that supported the achievement of its students. However, it was not completely free of intrusion. I will also discuss how parents and staff fought the erosion of their program and felt *punished* by specific district policies and programs instituted to meet the terms of NCLB that they felt undermined students' ability to succeed.

"State Standards Are the Minimum of What We Do": Curriculum and Instruction Practices That Subvert the Constraining Effects of NCLB and Support Student Success

The humanities program, an integrated social studies and English curriculum, created and piloted by a teacher at OMS in 1985, was considered a cornerstone of the school. It offered the core humanities courses along with Advanced Placement and International Baccalaureate offerings that would also fulfill the English and social studies requirements for graduation. The 9th grade year was dedicated to becoming acclimated to the high expectations of OMS through the Introduction to Humanities course.

The class became a shared experience that bonded students and defined the school. It was often referred to as the boot camp, because it was tasked with emphasizing the skills needed for their next four years. Mrs. Scott and Mr. Springer were part of the social studies department and co-taught Introduction to Humanities. They discussed with me the ideas and cultural expectations transmitted through the curriculum. They felt that it served a higher purpose in that it helped students understand:

> [w]hy it's a privilege to be here . . . There's a certain responsibility that they have to have as a student here—to be respectful of others, to accept others, to respectfully question, to not just be satisfied by just doing the minimum . . . That it's ok to stand alone as long as you're very convicted, and you're not inappropriate or rude by standing alone.

OMS was notorious for its summer reading assignments that were part of the humanities curriculum. Each summer, including the summer prior to 9th grade, all students were required to read two books and complete an essay in preparation for the year. The assignment was worth approximately 250 points, half of their first semester grade, and gave students a taste of the hard work expected of them. The books chosen were usually college-level and set the tone as they re-emphasized the academic mission and goals of the school. Students I interviewed spoke with a sense of pride and accomplishment about reading Homer's *The Odyssey* in time for their very first day at OMS.

I observed the first block Introduction to Humanities course, which was taught in the red double- wide portable next to the school. The back half of the room was set up for the Socratic Seminar with tables arranged in a block O for discussion. The front half of the room was filled with approximately 50 tightly packed desks, the back of a chair jammed into the front of the desk behind it, row after row.

Each 9th grader carried around a large 3-inch binder with their last name on the spine. This binder was designed to hold all their notes, handouts, and materials for the course as well as important information for 9th grade. It was to serve as a reference for their entire academic career while at OMS, something they could go back to if they needed to refresh their memory about history of early man, the poetry of Ralph Waldo Emerson, or the procedures for the Socratic Seminar used in the majority of the humanities courses.

I observed this classroom on my very first day at OMS in October 2008. School had been in session for roughly one month, and I was immediately impressed by the level of discussion being generated so early in the year, the ability of the students to sustain engagement through multiple tasks, the ease at which college preparation skills were being taught to such a large group, and the expectations and responsibilities assumed by the students to prepare for class:

> *I walk in a few minutes late to first period as the teachers are making announcements and take a seat in the back of the class. Mrs. Scott is talking about the PSAT to be given next Wednesday, the X period of electives, and Project Mentor. There will be 2 days of shadowing to help them start thinking about internships.*
>
> *Ms. Riley, who replaces Mrs. Scott as she leaves for an appointment, instructs everyone to take everything off their desks and then walks them through taping together a timeline made from three worksheets. They pass tape dispensers back through the rows with little disruption. She asks them to think about history and when it began. I count 43 students, 17 male and 26 female, racially mixed. The room is decorated with posters of Shakespeare, Plato, Aristotle, Da Vinci, student art and masks.*
>
> *The packet is comprised of a timeline of early man and several articles about the discovery of early human remains. She asks again, "What is history to you?" and "When does history begin?" At least five hands go up each time: "when it started being recorded," "(history has) always been – not always recorded," "everything that has happened in the past." The second teacher, Mr. Springer, stands at the back of the room and interjects questions and makes additional points. There's a lovely sense of enthusiasm in his voice as he talks about history.*
>
> *They are learning to take notes. Students volunteer to read passages out of the packet, and she guides them to highlight appropriate information and define terms as they go. It's a lesson in how to study at OMS, and it also prepares them for college. I do notice though that an African American boy sitting up against the wall*

> *has his hand up constantly, but is never called on. The bell rings and everyone heads back to the main building.*

Each day I observed, the class took on a similar process involving a great deal of discussion and independent thinking coupled with practical college preparatory skills and a foundational knowledge base. The Ohio Graduation Test (OGT) was never discussed while I was in the classroom, and the 9th grade history curriculum provided little tested information on the OGT.

During the interview with both Mrs. Scott and Mr. Springer, I asked them to talk about how they negotiated state social studies standards and preparation for the OGT with their specialized curriculum. They perceived that it was the promotion of meaningful and relevant learning opportunities, not test-driven instruction, which supported student achievement on the test.

Humanities teachers at OMS perceived state standards as having limited to no impact on their classrooms. Mr. Springer candidly explained:

> I can't quote state standards. I know what they are, but I couldn't recite them to you, but I think all the standards are built in (to the curriculum) . . . *State standards are the minimum of what (we do).* (We do) a lot of higher level thinking and analyzing of literature and also discuss history, so the standards are in there, *if anything what we do is probably exceed even what the standards are asking*. It's not like we have a certain standard in mind when we are looking at Mesopotamia or Ancient Rome . . . Standards don't drive what we do, and I think the test scores show that the kids are still getting that (the standards) even without emphasizing standard this, standard that.

These teachers also perceived that NCLB and high-stakes testing had limited impact on their teaching, because the school's self-imposed and long-term overarching mission to prepare students for college already had them meeting and exceeding these standards. Mrs. Scott made clear that high-stakes testing historically had limited impact in the school:

> So when tests like the Ohio Proficiency Test came along in the 90s and then the Ohio Graduation Test, the only thing we've done in the humanities is look at the standards the first year that the test comes out and we make sure that we already do what is asked. If there appears to be a hole somewhere that we miss then we incorporate it into our curriculum as part of our embedded curriculum. And then we don't discuss it anymore. It just becomes part of what we do. Students don't hear us say anything about the OGT hardly ever, because our goal is not to scare them about the fact that they have to remember on Wednesday October 13 that this will be on the OGT. We want them to understand the cause and effect of history and analysis of literature and historiography. If they're getting the

> skills that we think are preparing them for college we believe we've set the curriculum to where it's embedded for the OGT standards.

When asked why OMS students did so well on the OGT in comparison to the majority of other schools in the district that were intently focused on the test, they argued that the strict adherence to the benchmarks and the pressure of the OGT undermined other students and other schools. OGT preparation, characterized by a lack of context for knowledge and its dislocation from meaning and understanding, had limited ability to prepare students for the OGT and was perceived as "losing" students rather than capturing their attention and supporting learning. Mrs. Scott explained:

> I can tell you from experience at other schools and working with the social studies curriculum coordinator that [OGT test preparation] is all that is being taught . . . so if all that's being taught are GLIs (guided learning indicators) and benchmarks for the OGT then somewhere along the way those students aren't understanding why it's important to know it. When they walk into class in many high schools in this district, students will see on the board the actual indicator they're supposed to be learning today. So it gets lost, because it's not relevant, and it's definitely not interesting and meaningful.

This was proven by the fact that American History was tested on the OGT in their 10th grade year before students at OMS had a chance to take the United States History course in their junior year, yet they continued to do exceptionally well. Mrs. Scott again believed that it was the relevance that they instilled in the curriculum that allowed students to do well, even without specifically being exposed to the material:

> They have a whole year of American History and of World History in other high schools, and our students do not . . . We embed as much as we can of the American History that is required on the OGT, as strange as its sounds, to the Ancient course as well as World . . . if we're looking at the development of the government in Athens for democracy then we're going to study the types of government systems and economic systems which are OGT requirements . . . We just remind them that America, coming after these great civilizations, has mirrored many of the practices of these civilizations . . . *And it's meaningful. They understand it that way. And I can't speak to why they* [students at other schools] *are not doing well on tests, because they're exposed to the material . . . My assumption however is that it's just not relevant, the way it's being presented.*

Similar to Mr. Springer, other teachers perceived NCLB as a bottom-level benchmark. Mr. Hart, who taught 10th grade World History, 11th grade English and History, and AP US History, spoke at length about the limited effect of NCLB on his curricular and instructional practices:

Sara: Can you talk about how NCLB affects your teaching?

Mr. Hart: Yes. Not at all (with a laugh). I don't think that there has been a tremendous impact on what we do here . . . But in terms of my day to day practice *No Child Left Behind sets a bottom level.* Maybe, I don't know the relationship between NCLB and the OGT, because we gear some of our curriculum to the OGT but not a tremendous amount . . . if NCLB and the OGT are the bottom level, we're really shootin' at a much higher level. *On a daily basis very little impact on my teaching.*

Mr. Hart's content and instructional decisions were made with a great sense of autonomy and independence:

Sara: Is the content based on state standards? How do you decide what to teach?

Mr. Hart: Not really. For lack of a better pattern, it's driven somewhat by the textbook; what I have there (he points to a bookcase filled with binders that he has assembled on different historical topics) that would be meaningful for them, and what I can do . . . You have to make choices.

Sara: You have a binder that says civil rights and desegregation. So are those your choices or are they driven by something external?

Mr. Hart: *No those are my choices.*

Sara: What makes you decide you want to teach that material?

Mr. Hart: Certainly what I think is important. I know so much more history than I ever did, yet when I look at any particularly thing, I think I don't know enough. That leads me to constantly go back and rewrite it and if possible spend time on things that I think are important. *But it's all sort of self-driven.*

In sum, there is a great deal of pre-existing research and critical analysis of how NCLB narrowed the curriculum, promoted "teaching to the test," undermined teacher morale and efficacy, and perpetuated the achievement gap rather than closing it. In this study, policy is viewed as lived behaviors, or practices, that are part of the social context and fabric of OMS. Policies are both constrained and enabled by existing policy structures, but through negotiation, actors may find opportunities for resistance, refashioning, or reifying these.

The practices of curriculum and instruction as evidenced in the humanities classrooms provide examples of "policy appropriation" and "policy (as) practice" that help us to see how critical actors negotiate the constraints of policy in the context of everyday teaching and learning (Sutton and Levinson, 2001). As a form of policy negotiation, teachers determined the meaning of NCLB for their classrooms, and, in this case, it meant little to how they shaped their pedagogy. This meaning was socially contingent on the context of OMS. If it were not for its longstanding reputation as a high-achieving school with the test scores, graduation rates, and college attendance rates to support this reputation, teachers would not have had the power to negotiate policy in ways that preserved the humanities curriculum and college preparation focus of the school. Their student success afforded them a luxury of local control over their curriculum and teaching while other schools were being forced to follow pacing guides.

Teachers served as creative agents who took NCLB policy and melded it, or appropriated it, to meet the needs of their students. Their practices were examples of the pedagogical agency possible when teachers and schools make local decisions about how best to teach within the constraints of state requirements. As a practice, state accountability standards set a minimum benchmark for student achievement at OMS. College preparation and the expectations of the humanities curriculum superseded federal guidelines. Through their advanced coursework, the school set its own standards that both prepared students for standardized testing and graduation requirements and subverted the constraining effects of NCLB by holding themselves accountable to do more than "teach to the test." In this case, the requirements of NCLB had to be met, but they were otherwise insignificant to teachers or students. OMS measured its accountability based on college preparation, high expectations, and the meaningfulness and relevance of the curriculum to its students. OMS worked within and against NCLB to promote student achievement on its own terms.

However, OMS did not completely avoid the pressure of NCLB. The Columbus City School District was placed on Academic Emergency in 1998 and has struggled since to increase its graduation rates and test scores. Two of the ways the district attempted to do this was through enforced test preparation and credit recovery. Participants viewed these initiatives as harmful, demoralizing, and punishing to their school.

How to Punish What Really Works

OGT Preparation

In spite of the school's excellent rating by the Ohio Department of Education (ODE), accountability stood outside the door of each classroom. For staff there was an internal pressure to always do better, as Mr. Fisher explained:

> We tend to get higher passages on standardized tests. But here its not just passing, it has to be superlative. So if we're at a 91, then why aren't we at a 92? If we're at a 92, how dare we go back to 90.

Mrs. Altman agreed that the entire faculty was expected to share in the concern. They held staff meetings at the start of the school year to look at the test score data and discussed how to improve particular sections of the OGT. The idea was that all staff would come together to address the issue:

> I understand you're an art teacher, but the discussion today is how are we going to improve this section of the OGT. We're not hitting it for some reason. Why do you think we're not hitting it? What can we do?

She goes on to clarify that it is not just about test scores or the reputation of the program. It was also about real students and the potential of failing high school.

> You want the kids to have the basics. You want your program to do well. And you want as many kids, because if they don't pass the OGT they could conceivably not graduate for now, of course, those benchmarks may be changing. You don't want [that], none of us wants [that], that's heartbreaking and stressful.

However, concerns about those not passing the graduation test shifted resources and promoted lowered expectations back to what Mr. Springer referred to earlier as "the bottom level" or "the minimum of what we do."

Teachers discussed how in the early years of the graduation test, OMS attempted different strategies to help fully prepare students coming from the different middle schools with different academic backgrounds. Early on the humanities program, they tried to supplement the curriculum with direct OGT preparation. Mr. Hart discussed how, in spite of the fact that students generally scored well in social studies, the school sacrificed a unique Wednesday curriculum to OGT preparation, which he found to be a "dreadful" and difficult experience for teachers and students alike:

Sara: Are you under the gun to generate tests scores?

Mr. Hart: For whatever reason our OGT test scores have been really good. We've worked on improving them, and we've worked on coming up with new ways of using particularly the Wednesdays. When I first came here, Wednesday class used to be your area of interest . . . People did all these really interesting classes based on their own interests. Once OGT became an issue we were faced with [that] our freshmen and sophomore curriculums don't teach American History. We had to find a way to prepare them for that test . . . We took the components and tried to work it into the regular curriculum and then we used the Wednesday class to teach the things that were left over. So, basically, we would teach American

History from the industrial age to WWI, through the progressive era and a few topics. *It was dreadful.*

Sara: Dreadful?

Mr. Hart: *Painful.* It would start out that the first few weeks were ok. The freshman were still figuring out what this Wednesday thing was, but by the middle of the school year, the curriculum is completely different from the rest of the week and it was like "you have to remember American History again now." Just a lot of pressure all to meet the OGT. This year we ended up just teaching the regular curriculum. We'll take those pieces and work them in. But if you take a look at the test scores on the OGT the reason we can do that is our test scores are so much better than the district.

Even though Mr. Hart did not feel he was under pressure to produce test scores, he still experienced the "dreadful" and "painful" toll of accountability on his classroom and his teaching. This discussion stood in stark contrast to his comments in the first section of this chapter where he described the personal choice and freedom he experienced as a teacher at OMS. When the school attempted to take on NCLB on the state's terms, teachers and staff experienced the punishing, painful, and dreadful effects of accountability.

Dr. Steele, the parent of a sophomore, described her daughter's experience with OGT preparation. Like Mr. Hart, she characterized this diversion from the normal OMS curriculum as painful:

> In their freshman year, last year, since the freshmen are the only ones not having internships, Wednesday was OGT prep day. They had these classes in every subject that were designed to cover the things on the OGT that are not part of the normal curriculum, because OMS' curriculum is different from all the other high schools. *My daughter found it excruciating.* They'd have sessions on statistics, certain aspects of American History that don't get taught until later. They did try to do this in a sort of logical way working through history. I have no idea. The kids are very stressed about it, I know.

What Mr. Hart and this parent found painful and punishing was the interruption of interesting and meaningful curricula for test preparation "that is completely different from the rest of the week," made up of "leftovers" and lacking context. Both students and teachers found this appropriation of NCLB policy to be punishing to their curriculum and interests, creating a source of stress for teachers and students.

Dr. Steele explained that she was disgusted by the impact of NCLB on public schools and placed responsibility for the failure of schools back on the system itself:

> But the system is insane. It [OGT] just seems like this stupid hurdle that obviously if the classes are sufficiently rigorous, and the kids are getting graded, and they weren't doing credit recovery then we wouldn't have graduation tests. Then you would simply have to have passed a certain number of courses. *The fact that we have to even have such a test just goes to show that the system itself is failing.*

When the OMS community embraced NCLB on the state's terms, a shift in concerns occurred from talk of meaningful curriculum and relevant pedagogy to the "basics," test scores, and graduation rates. It created tension in the faculty, forcing those teachers and subjects outside of the tested curriculum to be held accountable for finding solutions for increasing student scores. It drove a school already successful in getting students to college to question its trusted curriculum and sacrifice it momentarily to test-driven outcomes. Participants including parents and students found the experience to be excruciating, painful, dreadful, and therefore punishing.

OMS also had to navigate credit recovery, another punishing district initiative to increase graduation rates. They argued it was detrimental to their students as well as all students in the district.

Credit Recovery

Credit recovery, a computer-assisted program used by Columbus City Schools to allow students to "recover" failed courses and increase graduation rates, was identified by many parents, teachers, and staff as a source of contention between the school and the district. Credit recovery provided eligible students with online versions of traditional high school courses that they could take for credit if they failed to pass in the classroom. OMS made it available after school in a computer lab. As Mr. Fisher explained, the district instituted credit recovery to meet a bottom-line goal of increasing graduation rates as dictated by NCLB:

> Whatever boosts the graduation rate, because that's our [the district] number one goal. So if that's your number one goal everything else falls in line with that. And if credit recovery is approved and lets you [the student] do that then that's what they are going to do. That's been a whole other can of worms.

He felt that as the district and schools fell in line behind this goal, students too fell in line with these lowered expectations. As Mrs. Altman explained, credit recovery lessened their ability to promote academic engagement:

> For a while there we felt like credit recovery undermined our program somewhat, because things that were rights of passage that you had to get through you don't have to get through to stay here anymore . . . They

> could fail and go to North Adult, but they had to pay $100 bucks and go to night classes and be there every night as opposed to now staying here after school for a free program on the computer. *But if kids are at risk for any reason they have a greater likelihood of choosing that path of least resistance. And kind of hand in hand with that, our ability to put their feet to the fire has diminished somewhat.*

By "rights of passage," she was referring to the humanities program and the skills and high expectations students learned in that classroom. She also talked about how credit recovery undermined graduation rates and failed students by creating the illusion that students could put passing off until they were near graduation. As a result, graduation rates slightly decreased at OMS:

> In the past, you get tired of going to night school or summer school, you get so far behind that it hits you in the face. What credit recovery does is it gives you the idea, sometimes the illusion, that you can make this stuff up, that time is on your side, that you can make it up. That's not true. That's affected our graduation rates, because kids put it off. This year especially, it's gotten more difficult, it's gotten more rigorous, so they're not flying through it.

A parent agreed that credit recovery served as a mechanism to inflate graduation rates that undermined the excellence of OMS:

> It has something to do with the greater culture in the city of Columbus, which doesn't expect excellence and doesn't seem to particularly value excellence. They value achievement, and even at OMS, and it's an issue where graduation rates I think are inflated because of credit recovery.

Parents were extremely agitated, because at the time of this study, if a student passed a course using credit recovery it was not indicated on the transcript that colleges reviewed for admission. Parents were angered by the possibility that a student could graduate from OMS, possibly with credit recovery, and that their transcript would be valued in the same way as a student who passed 9th grade humanities or senior government in the classroom. Parents perceived that credit recovery ruined the integrity of the program and weakened the merit of an OMS diploma in the eyes of colleges and universities. They fought the district to have credit recovery removed from their school.

Dr. Steele argued that credit recovery was experienced more intensely at OMS as a negative influence, because it undermined the climate of high expectations. Like OGT preparation, it was punishing to students and teachers:

> At OMS it's a worse problem than most, because since the courses are really demanding, I know there are kids if they can get credit recovery

> for that course, who just accept from the beginning they're going to fail. Just sit there and put their feet up, get through the course, fail the course, and then take it through credit recovery and pass it. It's disruptive. It's not good in the classroom. It's demoralizing for the kids. It's tremendously demoralizing for the teachers.

She felt that credit recovery failed students, because it "shunted them through the system" without concern for actual learning:

> I think it's been a disaster. I understand the district's position on it, which is we've got kids at the school, they want the kids to pass, and they want the kids to graduate . . .
>
> It's very easy to pass courses through credit recovery. In general I think that they shouldn't be doing it. If a kid fails a course the kids should take the course again and pass it. The idea is not to shunt them through the system so we can say this many kids have graduated, but to make sure they've actually learned enough to function in the world.

According to parents that I spoke with, the district often argued that OMS needed credit recovery to provide those students coming in less prepared with other options if they continued to struggle at the school. Dr. Steele argued that if the district were truly concerned, they would be willing to pay for tutoring programs. Humanities teachers offered tutoring on their own time without compensation before and after school, and talked about how little time they had to help students who needed it. Dr. Steele shifted responsibility back to the district and criticized them for their failure to serve students appropriately:

> Now it seems to me that if the district is really concerned about kids who are flailing, rather than offering credit recovery, tutoring help should be coming from central administration since these are the people who are so concerned that we have kids coming into OMS that are not academically prepared for it and are failing courses.

But she also felt, like others, that credit recovery made it unnecessary for students who did not want to be at OMS to leave, and that their disruptive attitude impacted the academic climate:

> You see it with the foreign language classes, because there's no credit recovery for foreign language classes. You see those kids take Spanish II again and again and again. Finally getting a teacher who's easy enough to pass them. My own position would be that we simply shouldn't allow it. Offering kids support, offering kids tutoring, contexualizing why the courses are so hard, and then accepting the fact that some people are going

> to transfer out after freshman year to give them the support they need so that if they want to lottery into another school they can do it. And if the numbers are down at OMS then the numbers are down at OMS. You've definitely got, I can see it when I drop the kid off in the morning, there are kids that waltz into the building with no books. And I don't understand it, because I see my kid being weighed down. She just looks at me, well those are the kids that aren't really at OMS. They're just sitting through the day and doing credit recovery. Makes no sense.

Credit recovery was another district program instigated by the need to meet graduation rates under NCLB. It was a form of macro-level *policy as practice* that engaged power/knowledge relations which constructed the terms of the state within the constraints of accountability. As a local practice, it was perceived to greatly impede curriculum and instruction, and deeply weaken the climate of high expectations by offering "a path of least resistance." Rather than increasing graduation rates, the policy in practice decreased graduation rates by creating the illusion that students could fail and quickly make up their classes toward the end of their high school career. This path of least resistance was perceived to undermine the climate of high expectations and the college preparation that served students so well. Credit recovery was a practice utilized by the district to "shunt" students through the system rather than attend to their academic needs and ensure they were adequately prepared for life after high school.

It was quite difficult to locate information about credit recovery through Columbus City Schools (CCS). However, PLATO Learning, the company that supplies CCS with its credit recovery software, highlighted the district in an August 2009 report (PLATO Learning, 2009). In this efficacy report, PLATO cited CCS as one of five large districts that have used their course completion and credit recovery software to improve their graduation rates and status under NCLB.

PLATO Secondary Solutions touts itself as "an evidence-based, technology mediated tool" to "power student performance gains" (PLATO Learning, 2009, p. 15). The company attributes the "success" of CCS to the use of its program, and success is defined in terms of standards and accountability. CCS began using PLATO in 1999 while placed under Academic Emergency by the ODE. In 2003 CCS piloted credit recovery in 10 high schools and then expanded to all 18:

> By 2003, the district's report card status improved from "Academic Emergency" to "Academic Watch." Following that success, Columbus City Schools implemented the Columbus Virtual High School, Credit Recovery Program, and various summer programs. In four years, graduation rates increased from 56% to 73.9%. In 2006–2007, the district's report card status advanced to "Continuous Improvement." The district aspires to exact a 90% graduation rate by 2012.
>
> *(PLATO Learning, 2009, pp. 13–14)*

NCLB and credit recovery shifted definitions of success to the terms of the state, those of graduation rates and test scores. Under NCLB, it is the numbers that matter, and the means of getting to these numbers are of little concern. How students get to graduation and what knowledge they leave high school with, whether it is college preparedness and a sense of empowerment or a passing score and a diploma, are of no consequence. Whether or not they have "learned enough to function in the world," what matters are the numbers and the district rating. OMS was deeply concerned about the means of their students' education, and credit recovery shifted the terms of educational engagement for their students. Some students engaged on the state's terms and measured their educational success with minimal standards, i.e., a passing score and a diploma. This undercut the terms of success OMS had laid out for its students.

Another Way to Punish a Good Thing: Overcrowded and Under-Resourced

When parents insisted that credit recovery be removed from OMS for the reasons above, they were accused of being elitist. "They (the district) think it's elitist . . . to say no credit recovery at OMS, but credit recovery at other schools." The district superintendent was very protective of educational equity and access students of color had to excellent schools. One year, CCS increased the number of freshman entering OMS through the lottery to 250 to alleviate some of the public pressure for increased access. However, the district decision to increase enrollment without increasing teachers or resources impacted the school's ability to maintain its program and was perceived to have an extremely negative effect on the culture of the school and the achievement of students.

As a high-profile school, from time to time the lack of access would leak out into the media. An editorial in the Columbus Dispatch questioned why the district did not put its energy toward replicating the program and criticized it for not providing more opportunities for its students. As Mrs. Cowan explained, it was perceived that CCS was trying to respond:

Sara: Why did OMS accept more freshmen?

Mrs. Cowan: People like it! Just like what you said. When you ask them "what's the best urban city school in Columbus?" they are probably gonna say Ohio Magnet School, because we receive a lot of honors. And I think because of that, people want us to accommodate more. And I think that it was the thought that we can make them larger. Let's accommodate some people . . . Let's bring it up to capacity, and let's make it available to more students.

For the most part, the parents that fought the most for increased access were predominantly white parents, those on the PTA and those out in the community, who had seen or felt the effects of having a gifted or academically driven student lose in the lottery. These parents put pressure on the district to open up more seats for their students, who they often referred to as "the kids that want it the most." Parents felt that "kids that really want to go to OMS should be given priority, and one measure of how badly you want to go to OMS is how successful you've been in school, in middle school, how hard you've worked."

The increase the freshman class created an overcrowded school that actually limited student access to the curriculum and jeopardized instruction. Mr. Carmichael was an active African American PTA parent whose son was a freshman. He told me increased enrollment physically prevented his son from receiving classroom instruction:

> They admitted 226 and half the time my son told me *he was in the hallway*. Not because he got there late, he was just standing there and the classes would fill up whatever amount of chairs there were. Although he could hear what was taking place, he and one or two other kids, *rarely was there enough space for all the students*. So that was a concern for me, that they accepted so many without making adjustments.

Mr. Carmichael also felt that the teachers' ability to serve students was limited by the increase in enrollment:

> It's even bad to put teachers in that position . . . Because if you're just going to put teachers in a position where they can't give writing assignments, can't give projects, because they don't have time to get to it. And even when they do give writing assignments . . . just for instance, it takes over a month, month and a half to get it back. I'm not critical of the teachers. I've asked them, and they've said, and I might be passionate now but I try to be levelheaded, and they say "we're trying to get to it, but we have a lot of students." And I understand that.

The lack of resources to serve the increase impacted the school. Mrs. Scott cut to the chase when giving her opinion on the increased enrollment, "We agree more students should have access to the program. What we don't agree with is not getting additional staffing to match it."

It was believed that the failed attempt to fix demand with increased enrollment and the fall-out from this led the superintendent to revert back to previous admission numbers. According to Mr. Carmichael:

> The superintendent comes to OMS every once in a while, and she [the superintendent] did mention that year they really wanted to open the doors to more, because they knew there was a great demand to be at a place like

> OMS, and they really wanted to try that out. *But they saw that the scholastic infrastructure couldn't hold that many so they kind of scaled back a lot.* But I think he [Mr. Carmichael's son] has to endure that his whole 4 years.

The adverse reaction of parents to the overcrowding and ways in which increased enrollment limited course offerings then placed further pressure on the district to rectify an already tense issue. As Mrs. Scott explained:

> Normally we would have about 180 freshmen each year, and the last three years that began to balloon to 220 without any new staff. Last year was the biggest year. And then as a reaction to parents being upset that no new staff was being added, and obviously that means overcrowding in classrooms as well as course offerings aren't as frequent, the district reacted with this program of OK we'll give a little bit of a separate category again in a lottery system now not based on racial background but academic profiling.

The inability of OMS to shore up the district's attempt to meet demands for increased access without increasing support eventually gave way to a long-sought selective admission program, which would admit 50 students based on merit before the regular lottery. Teachers surmised that the district hoped that an influx of academically motivated students would make it easier to manage a larger population:

> When you get 30 and 40 extra freshmen for 2 years in a row and no new teachers something's got to give. And something gave last year. And the concession was the selective lottery for (another lottery school) and OMS as well as a limit on the freshmen coming in to let us catch up.

Parents, teachers, and staff perceived that OMS was at the bottom of the district's priority list. The pre-lottery was one of the few times they felt the district had made a decision that supported their program.

Conclusion

The experiences of OGT preparation, credit recovery, overcrowding, and limited resources demonstrate what it means for schools and districts to play the accountability game on the state's terms. On more than one occasion, the district shifted responsibility to the school by increasing their lottery enrollments without increasing teaching staff or infrastructural resources, and then undermined the climate of high achievement by enforcing OGT preparation and credit recovery.

The push for accountability created similar constraints experienced by other less successful schools in the district, which hindered rather than supported their ability to promote student achievement. These schools' inability then to play the accountability game on the state's terms of graduation rates and test scores produced them as unsuccessful. OMS paradoxically played the accountability game on its own terms, re-appropriating a climate of high expectations and college preparation as achievement benchmarks, to subvert the constraining effects of NCLB. Its success at playing the game while not sacrificing excellence for achievement was what attracted parents and students.

However, rather than receiving additional support, infrastructure, or resources, the school was further burdened by the system's inability to provide an adequate education. The district placed money, time, and effort into OGT preparation and credit recovery rather than learning from its most successful school. In many ways, OMS was exploited and punished for being successful.

This chapter demonstrates the complicated negotiations schools face under NCLB. OMS worked within and against educational policies to attempt to both meet standards and recuperate from the losses it experienced from the "insanity" of the system. It is through these continuous struggles to refashion and re-appropriate policy on its own terms that OMS has managed to retain some of the joy of teaching and learning.

References

Darling-Hammond, L. (2007). Race, inequality, and educational accountability: The irony of "no child left behind." *Race, Ethnicity, and Education, 10*(3), 245–260.

Fusarelli, L. D. (2004). The potential impact of the No Child Left Behind Act on equity and diversity in American education. *Educational Policy, 18*(1), 71–94.

Gay, G. (2007). The rhetoric and reality of NCLB. *Race, Ethnicity, and Education, 10*(3), 279–293.

Hursh, D. (2007). Exacerbating inequality: The failed promise of the No Child Left Behind Act. *Race, Ethnicity, and Education, 10*(3), 295–308.

No Child Left Behind Act, 20 U.S.C. § 6301, (2001).

PLATO Learning. (2009, August). *PLATO Learning Secondary Solutions: An Efficacy Report* (Descriptive White Paper). Bloomington, MN: PLATO Learning.

Sutton, M., and Levinson, B. A. U. (Eds.). (2001). *Policy as Practice: Toward a Comparative Sociocultural Analysis of Educational Policy.* Westport, CT: Ablex.

THE WINTER DANCE

There are already students seated at the front of the auditorium. The 11th grader from Mr. Fisher's class with the three-year-old son, Raquel, directs parents to the orchestra pit. The energy is palpable as more and more students pour into the room. This is the first time I see the whole student body at one time, with the exception of 9th graders who are excluded from the assembly, because the auditorium is too small to hold the entire school.

Seniors want to be in the middle section. The Assistant Principals are repeating this over and over, and eventually one says it over the loudspeakers. There is a huge response—shouting and cheering, and booing. I see a young African American male in a tie and dress shirt stand up and start pointing and yelling at underclassmen to move. IT IS SO UNBELIEVABLY LOUD IN A SCHOOL THAT IS ALWAYS QUIET! I've not known this kind of noise at OMS.

The burgundy velvet stage curtains are lit by a nice set of stage lamps hanging from the ceiling. There are two limp fichus trees at the corners of the stage, and a podium sits stage left. It takes almost 25 minutes to seat the 10–12th graders and make everyone happy. The Assistant Principal says, "We have guests. Please be respectful and be quiet like you were asked," but the students are reluctant to quiet down. You can hear the restraint in his voice, trying to keep it together in front of the parents.

Dr. Davis starts the ceremony. Male and female attendants for the sophomore and junior classes enter from off stage. Both white and students of color are running for homecoming court, but it is predominantly African American students on the stage. The school cheers as each student's name is called. Cameras flash. I can almost guess the winners based on the applause. They stand spread out across the stage, alone, with lights shining down on them, to be measured and evaluated by their classmates. There's a variety of attire from casual to Sunday best. Esther from Mr. Hart's class is on the stage for the juniors. Her hair is now blazing red and she's wearing shiny black boots with a stiletto heel. She waves at everyone, her long acrylic nails dancing in the air. The boy who gets the loudest cheers from the sophomores is dragging himself across the stage with an ornery smirk. He's wearing probably what he wears every day—a loose t-shirt, baggy jeans, and sneakers.

Mrs. Scott takes the podium. She states that it's a tradition for the seniors to enter from the back of the auditorium and walk down the aisle. R&B music comes in over the loudspeakers and two names are announced. A mass of senior students sitting in the first eight center rows jump up cheering and pull out their cameras. They announce the first pair of names. Girls go down my aisle, boys down the other.

The senior girls are all wearing formal attire. One boy has taken a humorous approach, his pants hoisted up by suspenders, fake buck teeth, and taped glasses. There are two white males, two Black males, and five Black females running for the senior court. Back tattoos peak out from behind the austere appearances—a floor length teal spaghetti strap dress cinched in the front with a rhinestone clasp, a thin burgundy formal more appropriate for spring with an open back, a short, black casual dress—all appear to be wrinkled and worn, maybe from riding on the bus and dragging the hems through the wet and snowy parking lot.

The last girl descends in what looks to me like a second-hand wedding dress, heavy cream satin, embroidery and rhinestones, satin buttons down the back. I am taken aback by both the formality and ill-fit. The students are cheering the most for this young lady, cameras are flashing, and they are going wild. Her male counterpart wears a bow tie and old school football sweater. She is most definitely the star of this show.

As they descend, Mrs. Scott tells the audience about each student, their college plans, their favorite classes, their favorite high school memories, the people they respect the most, and the words they live by. The boys have written their scripts with humor, while most of the girls' memories and quotes are serious and sentimental. I'm struck by how almost every student mentions a member of the Humanities faculty as someone they most admire or their favorite teacher. Students say they are hoping to attend Cornel, Clark Atlanta, Wright State, OSU, Ohio University, Toledo University, Dayton, Loyola, Princeton, Boston College, Hampton University, York State, Tifton, Ashland, Urbana, Kentucky State. The boys attending Tifton, Ashland, Urbana, and Kentucky add that they are going to play football.

Staring at the court I acknowledge its diversity but also the fact that only three students are white. When I assess who is most excited, it's the front section of seniors. The majority of those students are Black. I am sitting in the back of the auditorium surrounded by white students who have no desire to cheer, stand up, or get out their cameras. While I do see groups of students racially intermixed, there are definite and distinctly large pockets of students of the same race sitting together and getting excited about this dance and others sitting together apathetically.

A few weeks after the dance I catch Dr. Davis in her office, and she updates me on the winners. So much strategy! The girl who was elected queen knew she was going to win, but she wants to be prom queen, and didn't attend the dance. The runner-up also did not attend due to her prom aspirations. The crown ended up going to the girl in the wedding gown. She was the 3rd choice. The school sprang for a dinner buffet that did not get eaten because the kids went out to dinner on their own.

Dr. Davis exclaimed, "There sure were a lot of white kids there. Where did we get all those white kids?" Turns out the white kids at OMS brought white kids from their home schools. She filled me on the rest of the court. The ornery boy from 10th grade won. All the white kids won. She says typically white kids have won in the past, because the (Black) vote is usually split. This year she said they (Black students) pulled together and made sure they got the queen nomination.

4

EXCELLENT INTENTIONS: RACIALIZED ENROLLMENT PRACTICES OF A SUCCESSFUL(?) URBAN SCHOOL

In a special issue of *Race Ethnicity and Education* (Leonardo, 2007b) authors argued that No Child Left Behind (NCLB) was in and of itself a racial project, and not merely a set of policies aimed at closing the achievement gap, but in actuality policies heavily invested in the larger racial system of the US. According to Leonardo:

> Overtly, it implicates improvements for students of color in its four targeted subgroups. Implicitly, NCLB is part of a racial project since it is enacted within a racialized nation-state. As part of the racialized state apparatuses, schools bear the markings and carry the anxieties of US race relations.
>
> *(p. 241)*

Leonardo (2007a) argues that "NCLB is whiteness turned into policy" (p. 275) and traces how NCLB is invested with, perpetuates, and reifies an educational system of white privilege. According to the author, NCLB promotes a color-blind ideology that attempts to obliterate race. As discourse it is a relation of power and knowledge that explains away racialized structural inequalities that have led to the systematic disadvantaging of students of color and high poverty. It is characterized by a belief in the declining significance of race and racism, situating inequalities as isolated incidences perpetuated by individuals that are ignorant, irrational, and pathological. It also individualizes success and failure, and blames people of color for the failures attributed to them. It downplays institutional racism and emphasizes racial progress, and downplays, ignores, or finds outdated the history of US slavery and genocide as important for understanding the US as a raced society (p. 267).

As such, Leonardo helps us understand how NCLB as a mechanism of color-blindness recreates, retraces, and fences in achievement as a white privilege. The impression of de-raced standards bear the absent marker of whiteness that dominates accountability (Demerath, 2009). Race is both meaningless and meaningful—failure of minority and disadvantaged students is blamed on individuals and cultures, but long-standing white achievement is based solely on merit. Achievement as a deracialized notion carries with it this absent white marker, while failure is racialized and individualized. As such, minority students *can fail on their own terms, but they cannot achieve on their own terms.*

This chapter looks at the ways in which Ohio Magnet School (OMS), in spite of its best intentions to be otherwise, deracialized achievement, racialized failure, and compromised equity for the sake of perceived excellence. I will look at how a pattern of racial inequality within the school was perpetuated, and how this unintended yet still highly consequential practice was explained by teachers and parents. Adults were concerned about the imbalance between students of color and white students as they accessed academic opportunities, and as we will see, though their intentions were to help all students be successful, their actions were more racially invested than they might appear to be. I will demonstrate how discourses of color blindness, disadvantage, and meritocracy were intricately intertwined with static constructions of urban educational identity and white privilege to produce and sustain the practices that allowed such inequalities to go on without real resolution.

Colorblind

It became apparent during my classroom observations that enrollment at OMS was stratified by race across the three college preparatory programs at the school, those being basic college prep, advanced placement (AP), and international baccalaureate (IB) programs. Of the classrooms I observed, IB courses were predominantly filled with white students, AP courses were also predominantly white with a slightly larger percentage of African American students, and college preparation courses like the combined English and US history course (a.k.a. "the split") were almost entirely African American (see Figure 4.1).[1]

When I began to talk with other faculty, staff, and parents about the overrepresentation of Black students in the college prep program, conversations typically took two paths. In one version of the conversation, race held an absent presence; participants talked around race, never clearly identifying it, but signifying it in the context of the discussion. The second version was a conversation peppered with discomfort and agitation at my raising the issue. Some participants resisted answering questions directly, often positing other possibilities for the stratification. Other participants openly expressed their agitation with me for asking. In all conversations, particular discourses circulated rendering race an (im)possibility for explaining the enrollment patterns. The following interview excerpt

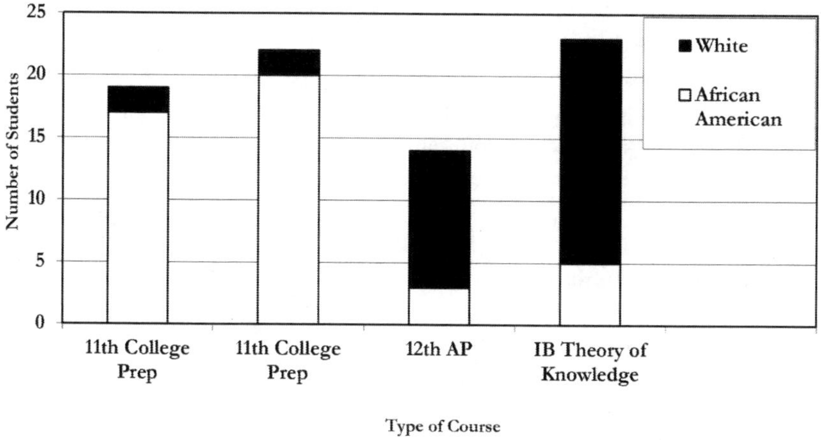

FIGURE 4.1 This bar graph represents the racial breakdown of a random sampling of four social studies courses at OMS in 2008. It demonstrates the trend of overrepresentation of Black students in the basic college preparation courses and an overrepresentation of white students in the Advanced Placement and International Baccalaureate courses.

offers an example of three of the dominant discourses at work at the school—a discourse of individual choice or meritocracy, the discourse of colorblindness, and the simultaneous raced and de-raced discourse of urban student identity.

Sara: Can you talk about why you think enrollment across the three programs is stratified by race?

Vice Principal: I just think that it's offered to the general population, and *I believe you just have more Caucasian kids that are interested in it.* It's not to say we don't have African Americans and other nationalities in there, because we do. It's just not the same component as far as numbers. But the kids that are African American have done really well and they benefit. *What people should look at is the rigor of the program and not the color of the race involved in it.* Because it's whether or not the individual, and *race doesn't have anything to do with being an individual,* whether or not they want to put in the time and the effort and the rigorous academics that it takes to get through the diploma program. And I think the people from outside will look at numbers and say "ohhh" (pitching his voice higher and with sarcasm).

Sara: Well I guess I was surprised.

Vice Principal: You've got more white kids in there than Black kids. What's wrong with the program (with same sarcasm)?

Sara: I guess I was surprised because the school is predominantly African American in general, so when I went into IB . . .

Vice Principal: *It's a personal thing on whether or not you want to work that hard. And that's where it is. And I don't think that's race based.* And I think that's individual. Whether you want to write a 4,000 word extended essay, whether you want to do the internship thing, giving back to the community is huge. Take the time to do Theory of Knowledge. You better be prepared for that.

This conversation occurred at the close of an interview I conducted with the Vice Principal just before school ended in June. He became agitated when I asked him to discuss the stratification of enrollment at the school. As evidenced above, the fact that more white kids were in the AP and IB courses was believed to be coincidental. He shifted responsibility to the students, asserting that the make up of the programs was a result of individual choice based on a student's willingness to put in the time and effort required, and coincidentally "you just have more Caucasian kids that are interested in doing it." He also asserted that I should not be looking at the "color of the race involved" in the programs, but the rigor required. He mocked my questioning during the interview with a great deal of sarcasm, indicating that I was unnecessarily critical.

This interview excerpt illustrates the ways in which a colorblind discourse was instituted along with the discourse of individual choice as justification for the overrepresentation of Black students in the college preparatory program. The choice discourse shifted blame away from the school and onto the students. It is connected to the story of meritocracy so inherent in US educational contexts, which we see in the Vice Principal's comments about IB students being those who had an individual desire to work hard. The colorblind discourse of race similarly worked to evade the pattern of racialized enrollment at the school, asserting that racial patterns were coincidental, and therefore not worth investigating. In effect, these kinds of explanations delimited any need to look harder at the issue. The school then was not held accountable for the patterns of inequality.

The next section looks at how the overrepresentation of African American students in the college preparatory courses at OMS was practiced and explained by faculty and staff, white students and parents, and students of color.

Faculty and Staff Explanations and Practices of Racialized Enrollment

The guidance counselors emphasized that as students progressed, they had "more and more choices" in terms of course taking each year. By junior year, students were able to take both AP and IB courses across the curriculum. Though I believe they felt they had students' best interests at heart, I found that faculty and staff in many ways dissuaded students from registering for these courses in practice. African American students were the most impacted by practices of recruitment and course registration.

Crash and Burn

Students were required to complete an application if they wanted to schedule AP or IB courses. Applications were not intended to exclude students, but to be used as a tool for counseling them. Both applications assessed prerequisite courses and requested grades, though neither program had a grade point average requirement. However, an analysis of the language used on the applications demonstrated that they had a second unintended function of discouraging students from scheduling these courses based along lines of race and class.

Both applications emphasized challenge, rigor, and "a serious commitment of time and energy well beyond that expected in a typical high school course of study" (IB application). For example, the AP application stated that success "occurs because of four key elements present *in the student and family*." These included a "strong desire to think critically . . . and to read and write," "*strong parental involvement* supporting student effort to achieve time management and patience with college-level curriculum," "student responsibility," and "academic *commitment* to the Advanced Placement experience *in the student's life*."

Each application asked a series of questions, which inadvertently encouraged students to sort themselves out of the courses. The IB application asked students to describe their study habits, if they had a job, and how many hours they worked, stating that, "It is strongly recommended that job hours be kept to an absolute minimum." Both applications ended with a signature page. For students, signing indicated a "commitment to work diligently," "desire for scholarship," and an understanding that both programs require exams at the end of the year for credit. Applications also required a parent signature, indicating that they understood the rigor and commitment expected as well. The AP application also stated that parents understood that classes were "equal to that which is expected of a college freshman," and that there is a financial obligation for calculators, review books, and materials.

These applications served as a deterrent for those students who had limited parental engagement. Though I did witness a short recruitment talk in Mr. Hart's English and US history course, the school held its information session in the evenings, and the counselors and teachers recognized how difficult it was to get more than the regular group of involved parents to attend these meetings. Jamie, an African American junior in Mr. Hart's class, explained that his "mom's not really the best academic person" and he depended more on people in his community for support (Student focus group, April 22, 2009). Natasha, an African American and Puerto Rican junior in Mr. Fisher's afternoon combined class who also held a full time job, explained that her mom worked nights and that "it would be kind of hard to ask my mom . . . to come to something . . . Its kind of hard for a parent to have to be involved with everything with their student if they're not able to be there." The emphasis on parental involvement immediately constituted a barrier for students who had limited parental support or engagement in their academics for numerous reasons.

It was also clear that the messages students received made them aware of the high academic expectations of the course, but unclear of the benefits. Students in the college prep program who did not take advantage of AP or IB discussed how the reputation of the courses discouraged them from applying. Natasha thought the school could do more in terms of explaining the benefits:

> Some teachers rarely explain what's in AP or IB. They'll say well it's a test at the end of the year. *It's work. It's work. You have to study*. That makes people not want to go to it. If you explain the advantages of it, like well it could benefit you later on; you could get this done, this done and this done with it. I think people would sign up for it more. If they realize what it could do for them they would sign up for it more.

Tanesha, another African American student in the 11th grade split course, agreed that the school failed to emphasize the benefits or "that you can learn and have fun . . . It's just telling you that . . . AP and IB is just work-work all the time."

Parents also thought that the school tended to emphasize the rigor of the courses over the benefits, and they perceived that students were weeding themselves out before they even applied. One white parent of a student in the AP program stated, "I would like to see more encouragement for (these programs)." In her experience, the guidance counselors were not:

> proactive in getting the information out and making parents understand what this program is and encourage everybody to try and go for it . . . Instead of putting up criteria that weeded out kids to begin with, let people apply who want to apply . . . but don't discourage them. Open up the doors for them.

Guidance counselors also tended to emphasize the rigor of the courses over the benefits. Mrs. Cowan used the size of the book to talk about AP European history, a sophomore course option. "I said it's taught like a college level course . . . I held up the textbook, because that sucker is big." She felt that it was a delicate balance between taking advanced classes and maintaining student success, and she wanted students to "try something different, but don't overload." Students and parents were, according to her, "clammering" for AP courses, but she felt that "For some kids it's wonderful, but for other kids it could be *crash and burn* . . . I think we just have to do a really good job as counselors and parents to make sure that we are selecting the right students." When I asked if she felt these scheduling decisions precipitated into racially stratified classes, she politely evaded the question, and said I may want to talk to the other counselor about that issue.

Starting at a Disadvantage

When scheduling students, the other guidance counselor, Mrs. Altman, said her main priority was making sure students met their graduation requirements and received their college prep diploma. Students had to complete the necessary prerequisites to enter AP and IB courses, and this depended on what courses they were able to take in middle school. Not all middle schools had the prerequisites needed for a student to hit the ground running at OMS.

I asked her how OMS helped students who did not have access to the appropriate prerequisite courses or recommendations needed at the middle school level to make them eligible for AP and IB. She stated that they could "accelerate through their sophomore year with the blocks [block scheduling], but they need to know that they need to accelerate through." She admitted though that accelerating was not always possible due to scheduling constraints, as "there's choices [between classes] that they're going to have to make, and sometimes things don't fit in terms of schedule." Students preparing for AP and IB took several classes together and continued on as a group throughout high school. As one student stated, "you have to have a background to come into a little track with some people who are similar to you." Unfortunately, this academic background tracked along lines of race.

OMS did not have clear intervention strategies to make sure that incoming freshman were made explicitly aware of how they needed to accelerate to take advantage of AP and IB. In talking to students, the lack of middle school preparation and limited knowledge of prerequisites was an obstacle to taking advanced courses. Students coming from traditional middle schools, as opposed to the alternative or "feeder" middle schools with prerequisites that aligned with AP and IB, suffered from limited access to needed classes, which further limited their opportunities in high school, and these students tended to be predominantly students of color.

Mrs. Altman also wanted students to "choose things that they're strong in, and they like, and they think will relate to their future path," but she also perceived that the "social dynamics" and "peer pressure" impacted students' desire to choose AP or IB and stay enrolled. "Different social groups have different pressures, so put it that way." When asked about the racial stratification of enrollment, she admitted the school was at least partially responsible:

> I think there's a variety . . . it's a very complicated mix of reasons why that occurs. *There are probably things that we could be doing to encourage kids more to take those academic risks, to seek out the rigor. Part of that is on us.*

Students I interviewed who were already in AP or IB, or had plans as freshman and sophomores to enroll, had some prior knowledge of the requirements. Eliza, an Asian American AP senior, did not experience any recruitment activities at

OMS, but knew of the options from middle school. Alexis, a white junior IB student, applied to the lottery as an upperclassman expressly to enroll in the IB program as it was the only one in the city. She and her father independently set up a meeting with OMS to learn more about the program and how to apply.

Of the five freshman students I interviewed during focus groups, four started their freshman year with intentions to enroll in one of the advanced programs, and some had already applied to AP European history for the sophomore year. Interestingly, three of these students came from a predominantly white and middle class neighborhood near the school and another student, who was African American, had attended a foreign language immersion school known for its academic excellence. As a result, they had the advantage of the appropriate prerequisites and recommendations from their middle school teachers to schedule pre-AP/IB chemistry in their first year.

In talking with them about their knowledge of prerequisites and their decision-making process for scheduling courses, African American students appeared to have scheduling issues that white students I interviewed did not. Erica, a freshman, explained that she wanted to take AP courses, but she was not aware of the requirements. She also felt she had been incorrectly scheduled for courses. Natasha as well appeared misinformed about her options for AP and had issues with her schedule. She stated that had she known Mr. Fisher, her favorite teacher, was going to teach AP English that year, she would have applied. She also signed up for AP physics, and, by her account, she not only had all the prerequisites for the course she also had good grades, "but for some reason . . . they didn't give me science this year. They just totally skipped me out on it."

As I talked to students, it became clear that students coming from traditional middle schools entered high school at a disadvantage, because they lacked knowledge about the programs and did not have access to prerequisites at the middle school level. For students like Natasha who wanted to take some AP courses like physics but were also still in the basic college prep courses like history, it was quite possible that, as Mrs. Altman alluded to earlier, the schedule created tracks that inhibited the ability to schedule courses in both college prep and AP programs simultaneously. It was also potentially easier to overlook Natasha's course request for physics, because, as I came to learn, she was identified as a college prep student with average grades who was perceived to be as disinterested in school. The rigid schedule and lack of availability of prerequisites at various middle schools inadvertently encouraged a tracking pattern of students into the three programs.

When Interests Converge

Historically, social studies teachers recognized that students of color were not taking AP courses. A previous AP teacher who had since left the school had a reputation for limiting the students in the course, because she was concerned about maintaining passage rates on the end-of-year AP test. According to one teacher, "Her class was never bigger than eight people. It's hard to justify having a year-long class with eight people and almost solidly white." It was acknowledged in abstract that the racial make up of the course was an issue, but it took a turn of events to prompt a response.

When the AP program began to lose students, teachers became concerned that the program would be pulled from the school, and a targeted effort was made to recruit more students in general and students of color in particular. As Mr. Fisher explained:

> So I felt like that in order to keep the class, and because of my own feelings about equity, I went out and recruited African American kids to take it who wouldn't have taken it otherwise unless I went and invited them in, and some white kids too, and a couple of Asian American kids who knew me . . . So they might not ordinarily take it, but I'll talk them into doing it, not only because I think they would benefit from it, (but) I am not worried about their test scores.

This move to recruit more Black students when the program was in danger of disappearing provides an example of "interest convergence" (Bell, 1980) as a daily practice of teaching and learning.

The principle of interest convergence posits that "the interest of Blacks in achieving racial equality will be accommodated only when it converges with the interest of whites (Bell, 1980, p. 523). Bell challenged the dominant narrative that the *Brown v. Board of Education* (1954) ruling, which declared segregated schooling unconstitutional, truly represented a moral and cultural shift toward equality. His analysis of *Brown* demonstrated that the decision was the result of the convergence of white self-interests with Black interests in racial equality. Bell (1980, pp. 524–525) identified three points of convergence for white interests and the passage of *Brown*. First, it was argued that passage would repair the tarnished reputation of American democracy due to slavery and segregation on the international front. Second, it offered reassurance to Black US soldiers returning from World War II that they would not face continued discrimination. Third, once it was realized that segregation served as a barrier to southern US industrialization, *Brown* was seen as converging with national economic interests.

Just as the moral imperative of "all men are created equal" was not enough to end segregated schooling, the recognition that students of color were discouraged from the AP program was not sufficient in and of itself to increase the enrollment of Black students. This is not to say that teachers' intentions were purely self-motivated. What this instance demonstrates is that it was the convergence of a more motivated interest in preserving the program with concerns for equity and access for students of color that brought about some change. Students of color began to be accommodated, because it was of benefit to the

AP program, but equity alone did not precipitate their recruitment. It is also important to recognize that even with these efforts, students of color were still underrepresented, and this is in part due to the discursive framings of urban identity that justified little more than a passive response.

Teachers also felt that recent attempts to expand the AP program had "watered down" the curriculum and instruction, because of a lack of criteria for admission. As a result, it was perceived that the classes were "more diverse and less successful" and engendered "less of a pure level of learning," because the program expanded without acceptance criteria.

Paradoxically Mr. Hart also recognized the benefits of having "lower-level" students in his classes: "If I ask a question in the (basic college prep) class it will generate discussion . . . If I ask a question in the AP class, and I'm very frustrated by this, there are six kids that discuss. That's it". Though Mr. Hart worked hard to keep students on task and manage disruptions, the students in the split course were always eager to participate. In the AP class, I watched those same six students he identified answer his questions over and over. I think it's important to note that even as more students were recruited for AP, it was not always viewed as beneficial to the level of excellence expected in the AP classroom, adding another complicated layer to how interests converge in schools when it comes to excellence and equity.

All of these mechanisms—preventing the crash and burn, entering high school at an academic disadvantage, and doing just enough when interests converge—are deeply connected to relations of white privilege that sustained the pattern. White parents also offered de-raced explanations for the benefits they received from the underrepresentation of students of color and poverty in the advanced classes.

Leaving "the Troublemakers" Behind

Of the 11 parents that I interviewed, 8 were identified white and 3 considered themselves African American. Of the white parents, all but one of their students, a freshman, were participating in AP or IB programs. Of the three African American parents, one student was taking one AP course.

White parents overwhelmingly talked about how the AP and IB courses made it possible for their students to leave the troublemakers behind. As one parent explained, "But as he got into his sophomore year and he could take AP art history and AP Euro, then the troublemakers were left behind. And now he's in IB and they're gone as far as I know."

There was a perception that OMS was attracting more and more students not interested in academics, because it was safe, or parents were choosing the school in good faith hoping that OMS would prepare their academically disinterested student for college. These students were perceived as negatively impacting the climate of the school, and AP and IB courses served to "weed out" the troublemakers. Parents perceived this weeding out process as a benefit for their own students:

> So that just showed me, well the more the students progress on to their next classes, so my son's going to be in AP classes, you're not going to see the kids that were troublemakers. If you do I'd be very surprised. The more he gets into school, and the more, the higher grade he gets, the less that becomes a problem. The first year it was a problem, there were disruptions. This year I don't hear that.

In these conversations, parents did not make a connection between their white student's escape to AP and IB and the predominantly African American students left behind in the college prep courses. The mechanisms of course enrollment, some well-intended and others creating unfortunate disadvantages, maintained the advanced programs as predominantly white, though the school would argue that this occurred inadvertently due to student choice. The advanced courses therefore became a form of white privilege and the property of whiteness.

According to Harris (1995), US society is based on a system of property rights located within racial subordination.

> Slavery as a system of property facilitated the merger of white identity and property. Because the system of slavery was contingent on and conflated with racial identity, it became crucial to be "white," to be identified as white, to have the property of being white. Whiteness was the characteristic, the attribute, the property of free human beings.
>
> *(p. 279)*

Through the slavery of Blacks and the seizure of Native American lands, whiteness came to be a form of privilege to ownership and a form of protection from being owned:

> Whiteness became a shield from slavery, a highly volatile and unstable form of property . . . Because whites could not be enslaved or held as slaves, the racial line between white and black was extremely critical; it became a line of threat of commodification, and it determined the allocation of benefits and burdens of this form of property. White identity and whiteness were sources of privilege and protection; their absence meant being an object of property.
>
> *(p. 279)*

Based on this historically sedimented relationship between whiteness, property, and protection, Harris identifies four property functions or rights ascribed to whiteness, which Ladson-Billings and Tate (1995, pp. 59–60) re-apply to the system of US education:

1. Rights of disposition in which whiteness as property is viewed as alienable or transferrable, such as the transfer of certain forms of white privileges to students who conform to white cultural practices and forms of knowledge production in schools.
2. Rights to use and enjoyment in which whiteness gives students access to the use and enjoyment of facilities, resources, and curriculums; resource disparities between affluent white schools and schools of color are one example.
3. Rights of reputation and status in which positive reputation and status are associated with whiteness, for example the reputations often associated with predominantly white and affluent private and public schools.
4. The absolute right to exclude which follows from the construction of whiteness as that which excludes markers of Blackness; segregated schooling is an example of the absolute right to exclude.

The property values of whiteness applied to the US educational context helps to explain how apparent racial inequalities of opportunity were not mere coincidences or the result of individual choice, but inherently produced by and productive of racialized power relations that make use of whiteness. Whiteness colored the enrollment process, and advanced curricula, status, and prestige became privileges from which white students could benefit more often than students of color, particularly because they were more likely to have attended middle schools that aligned with OMS. White students and families, due to inflexible scheduling that maintained tracks, their access to middle school prerequisites, and an early knowledge of requirements, maintained their rights to the use and enjoyment of the programs, while African American students were structurally excluded from this use and enjoyment. As predominantly white courses, they took on a positive reputation and status, one that was not bestowed on the predominantly Black college prep courses. The right to exclude, a component of white privilege, was inextricably bound up in the use of applications and an emphasis on rigor over benefit, which discouraged college prep students, students with jobs, and students with disengaged parents.

These practices were justified in and through racialized discourses of urban students that constructed them as disinterested in school, and allowed the school to overlook structural issues that may have impeded their desires to apply. De-raced urban student identity was a knowledge formation caught within power relations where colorblind discourses and the discourse of individual choice circulated to produce and preserve white privilege. These discourses maintained the absent presence of race, rendering race something visible yet inconsequential (i.e., we could see that classes had patterns along lines of race, yet these patterns were rendered insignificant). These articulations impaired any desire or need to look further, look structurally, or reflectively question practices that might be having an impact on Black students.

The choice discourse and the colorblind discourse were effectively articulated with urban educational identity. This articulation contained students within de-raced discourses of urban disadvantage and risk that worked in tandem with discourses of individual choice that allowed participants to evade socially and historically constructed racialized power relations circulating within the school. Students were constructed as individually responsible for their failure to take advantage of opportunities and colorblindness solidified this explanation, eliding race through beliefs that race no longer mattered in US schools.

(Not) Talking about Race

Shortly before I started my study, Dr. Davis began her position as Principal of OMS. She recognized that race was an issue. Her story about how a teacher broached the subject with her demonstrated how race held an absent presence in the school, something that was acknowledged by some, but not openly discussed:

> I had heard those things prior to coming. Someone said "oh, here are some issues you've got to face." So I thought, how do you talk about those concerns and if they truly are concerns . . . I have to give you a copy of this article. Someone put this article in my mailbox. It talks about basically increasing the minority presence in AP courses and what this teacher did to improve that. *And an AP teacher put this in my mailbox, so I thought, hmm, the door is open. I didn't have to come in (as a Black woman) and say guys you don't have enough Black kids in AP.* Someone in that AP department noticed that there were not enough. It was amazing that the teacher gave it to me, and when I talked with her about it . . . They know that they need more, and I've even talked to Mr. Fisher. I said if you guys know this, and I told him in the summer, what are you doing about it? *We can't just allow things to happen and we not do anything. Because there's nothing wrong with saying it.* And then we can go . . . some kids don't want to be in AP. Well why is that? What are we doing again to sell the AP program, to make the AP program more attractive?

As she assessed the situation, she recognized the need to talk openly about the school's responsibility in directing students to AP and IB and motivating them to believe in themselves:

> We're going to have a meeting with just the AP teachers and talk about *who are the kids, what do they look like, and I think those conversations have to be, we have to have them. Because I don't know who is making the choices* . . . well I'm sure the kids are choosing AP. I would assume that parents are pushing AP, and I would assume that counselors are directing to AP. *Sometimes we don't direct students as best as we could, and sometimes kids don't believe that they can meet the challenge.*

Teachers and staff had good intentions, but these intentions cut two ways. They wanted students to be successful academically and did not want to discourage students by placing them in courses that would prove too difficult. But they also intended to protect the excellence of their advanced classrooms. They were concerned about how expanding AP and IB enrollments would negatively impact classroom management, curriculum and instruction, and test scores. While applications overemphasized rigor and served to weed out those students who were not perceived as having the academic habits and family support necessary to succeed, staff and teachers recognized that they were not doing enough to invite students into the courses. Their excellent intentions to protect students from the "crash and burn" produced more dominant effects of discouraging students of color from taking the courses and continued the practice of an uneven distribution of students by race across the academic programs.

Dr. Davis wanted to address the issue head-on and followed through on addressing the concerns she raised in the interview. When I returned to the school in December 2009, she briefly mentioned some changes they had made to make the advanced courses more attractive as well as to improve the reputation of the college prep program so as to support the academic identity of students in that program. This was a step in the right direction; however, I expect that it is difficult to become completely unhinged from the historical and socially constructed practices and policies that maintain such systems of disadvantage. The next chapter looks more intimately at the ways in which students negotiated the discursive constructions of urban identity and fashioned themselves as subjects of their own educations.

Note

1 The numbers for Figure 4.1 are based on visual counts I took during observations. It is problematic to make assumptions about race in this way, but the point is to demonstrate the relative ratios of white students to students of color in each type of course.

References

Bell, D. A. (1980). *Brown v Board of Education* and the interest convergence dilemma. *Harvard Educational Review, 93*, 518–533.

Demerath, P. (2009). *Producing Success: The Culture of Personal Advancement in an American High School*. Chicago, IL: University of Chicago Press.

Harris, C. I. (1995). Whiteness as property. In K. Crenshaw, N. Gotanda, G. Peller, & K. Thomas (Eds.), *Critical Race Theory: The Key Writings That Formed the Movement* (pp. 276–291). New York: The New Press.

Ladson-Billings, G., & Tate, I. V. W. F. (September 01, 1995). Toward a critical race theory of education. *Teachers College Record, 97*(1).

Leonardo, Z. (2007a). The war on schools: NCLB, nation creation and the educational construction of whiteness. *Race Ethnicity and Education, 10*(3), 261–278.

Leonardo, Z. (Ed.). (2007b). Special issue on no child left behind [Special issue]. *Race Ethnicity and Education, 10*(3).

MAKING TROUBLE AT OMS

I sit on a stool in the corner by the computers and the chalkboard on the far side of the room. Students trickle in for the International Baccalaureate Theory of Knowledge course. Two boys sit near me, one white with thick curly hair wearing a soccer jersey and the other African American wearing a red t-shirt and loose shorts. As I'm making notes, the African American student holds out his hand and shakes very firmly. I tell him my name and smile as we wait for Mr. Westfall to start class. They don't know if I'm a student, a substitute teacher or what. The class is overwhelmingly white, and I take a quick count of what I see. It's not an accurate way to understand student identity, but it paints a picture of classroom life in this school: 5 white males, 3 African American males, 13 white females, 2 African American females, 1 Southeast Asian male, and 1 Southeast Asian female.

The white girls' IB "uniform" comprises skinny jeans, chucks, and cardigans stretched over the ends of their hands. They are all very thin and petite like birds, with the exception of one girl who is heavier and has a round face. The two African American girls are dressed more athletically, hair pulled back in a ponytail with a ribbon headband. The boys don't share a style of dress. It runs the gamut from jeans and dress shirts to loose cargo shorts, jerseys, and t-shirts. There are also kids I wouldn't expect to see in the IB class—a tall boy with blond tipped hair who looks like he would be more interested in being cool and playing basketball. When Mr. Westfall asks what is meant by the term "concentrated medium," this student gives a very in-depth answer.

Mr. Westfall is very experienced at getting the class under control by using his voice, and he never cracks a smile. To my surprise, these IB students talk quite a bit and require frequent reprimanding from their teacher throughout the entire class. Today they are going to have small group discussions about art: Is art a way of knowing? Do we learn things from art? Why don't we test art with the OGT? Then he introduces me and asks that I explain my research question and how I'm conducting my study. He says it's like a more complicated "EE" or extended essay, which is a requirement to complete the 2nd year in IB.

Mr. Westfall uses a deck of playing cards to divide the students into groups—kings, queens, jacks, and aces. Each group takes a white board to record their discussion, and they are scattered between two classrooms. I float around to see the different groups and then choose to sit with the group of the first two boys I met when I came into the class. The curly haired boy makes inappropriate remarks intended, I think, to be humorous. He asks, "Is sex art?" and then turns around sheepishly and exclaims to me "Please don't judge me!" I inform him that I'm just listening and observing. The conversation continues in this vein, a mix of off topic comments threaded with sexual humor.

Two groups in the main classroom are having very serious discussions about art. I hear a white female student in the back corner complaining with an tone of superiority in her voice that this exercise is going to be so boring, that everyone is going to agree that art is important, so she's going to disagree. She says it's blasphemy for her to take this position, because her "opa's an artist." A slip of a girl with dark hair and an annoyed lilt in her voice says, "What's an opa?" "Grandfather in German," the other replies. "I don't know German," the girl responds. Then she says, "I really don't think art is important." This sets off a passionate discussion. Another female student with long brown hair cut into a trendy style that many of the IB girls are wearing becomes suddenly very upset. "How is doing trig important to me if I'm going to be an artist! You're going to have a boring life. You're boring, because you don't like art!" They bicker back and forth, on and off for the next 30 minutes. Though they never raise their voices, something in the dagger looks they give each other makes me wonder why so much tension over a hypothetical question.

A quiet male wearing a black and white striped shirt, black skinny jeans, and black chucks attempts to jump into the conversation. The boy in the soccer jersey tells him with a major eye roll to stop being an "IB philosopher." Mr. Westfall leaves the room, and I see cell phones come out from pockets and flip open. When I ask about the new cell phone policy that forbids use in classrooms, they say nobody cares, nobody pays attention, and nobody follows it. Well at least not in IB I guess.

Class reconvenes and Mr. Westfall is trying to locate the groups. When he asks, "Where are the queens?" a Southeast Asian male student playfully raises his hand with an over the top smile and everyone laughs. Some of the laughs are in jest of him, but I am so impressed by his confidence. If he is bothered by the laughs that were at him and not with him, he didn't show it. I've seen this student before. He usually gets the male lead in all the plays and appears to be very outgoing. His downfall I suppose is that he likes to talk. I watch him chat over the teacher most of class. In spite of perceptions that students leave the troublemakers behind as they move into AP and IB courses, I found this classroom to be just as disruptive as any of the other classes I observed.

5

URBAN CACHET

This chapter looks at how Ohio Magnet School (OMS) staff, parents, and students negotiated urban identity to their advantage. In its transformation from predominantly white desegregation-era magnet school to predominantly Black urban success story, OMS developed a kind of "urban cachet," or prestige and uniqueness because of its urban-ness. Both Black and white families as well as the school exploited OMS' urban cachet to gain benefits in terms of grants, awards, and college scholarships. However, I believe Black families understood the politics of their negotiations while white families and school staff were less cognizant of the larger racial implications. Rather than disrupt taken-for-granted assumptions about urban students or challenge the victory narrative of success that required an always failing urban other, they used these representations to pull at the heartstrings of grant committees and college admissions officers. Urban cachet became a valuable asset, and I am not disagreeing with the use of that cachet to support students. What I am interested in interrogating are the effects of that cachet as it continued to position students as objects rather than subjects in their own educational lives. This chapter looks at three examples of urban cachet and the effects of appropriating urban identity.

Transformation, Promise, Breakthrough: Urban Cachet and the Construction of Students as Objects

The district was proud of OMS, and rightly so, because of the amazing success of its students. OMS was recognized in 2007 by the National Center for Urban School Transformation for its ability to transform the urban school setting into one "where all students achieve academic proficiency, evidence a love of learning, and graduate well prepared to succeed in post-secondary education, the workplace, and their communities." This was one of numerous and impressive accolades received by the school. The PTA expended a great deal of labor filling out applications, securing letters of recommendation, and putting together portfolios to ready submissions for awards like this one. The monetary prizes associated with these awards were used to purchase student resources that directly supported their achievement. These recognitions also gave them pride of place in the struggling district, a strong reputation that could be a bargaining chip with the school board, and visibility for students who were going on to college.

Most, if not all, of the awards and recognitions received by the school were hinged on its identity as a high-achieving urban high school. In this era of accountability where schools were measured by the test scores and graduation rates of their students, the reproduction of the urban educational other was a form of policy in practice, where schools such as OMS received credit and recognition for educating those students least expected to succeed. Simultaneously, the practice of capitalizing on urban identity was used to support students, making it possible for the PTA to shore up the under-resourced school. Yet, without its urban other, the achievement at OMS would not be so surprising or worthy of recognition. It is the expectations of low achievement from students of color, the discursive relations of whiteness/achievement and Blackness/failure, which give OMS its referential power.

Individual parents also managed and manipulated urban identity and cachet. When choosing a high school for their students, these parents expanded their decision-making criteria to include not only accountability and curriculum standards, but to also how they might further capitalize on the urban-ness of the school as a college entrance strategy and for personal gratification. I provide two examples.

"It's a Strategy": How African American Families Negotiate Urban Student Identity

Mr. Carmichael was an active member of the PTA and African American father whose sophomore son was reluctantly recruited to the Advanced Placement program. During the focus group, it was clear that Mr. Carmichael supported the school, but he referred to the curriculum as "watered down" and not of the same caliber as private schools in the area, like the one his daughter attended. He described how he perceived that Black parents such as himself were taking their kids out of private and parochial schools to capitalize strategically on the urban cachet of OMS.

According to Mr. Carmichael, these parents did not see themselves as "urban;" they were middle or working class parents with professional jobs living in or near middle class neighborhoods; they were educated, and if not college educated, they made up for this via engagement in their students' academic lives.

Mr. Carmichael explained what he perceived to be the decision-making process of parents he knew:

> You might not be as special at a private school, like at Academy or St. Charles. Even if your kid is doing As, at a lot of these schools you may have 20 kids with a 4.1. So depends on what the parent's goal is for that child, maybe the child might be aspiring to go to a certain school. The parent will say you're not special here . . . *My concern is that with the parents it's a strategy. I'll take my, maybe even A student . . . put them at (OMS) and they should sail through. And the schools (colleges) think "here's an inner city kid, look how well they've done with the opportunities they've had." Well, no they really (aren't an inner city kid), but that private middle school is not on the transcript so they (the colleges) don't see that. Every parent I talk to, to me it seems to be a strategy.*

However, teachers and students perceived that urban cachet made it "easier" for Black students to get into college, therefore they did not have to work as hard. One teacher spoke about a discussion he had years ago with some students as to why they thought the International Baccalaureate and AP programs were not as attractive to Black students. Race mattered according to these students, but Black identity was viewed as an enviable advantage as opposed to a disadvantage:

Teacher: Another kid said that Black students don't have to have as good of credentials to go farther, because they get all the minority advantages.

Sara: That's the perception?

Teacher: Well, no that's the truth. It's easier for them to get scholarships and get admitted to colleges. They don't have to stack their resumé nearly as much as the white kids do, because of the whole minority, informal affirmative action kind of thing. This is true . . . And [OMS is] a harder program so what's the point of doing that if you don't need to . . .

Sara: I wouldn't have expected that, not needing . . .

Teacher: Not needing to have the good stuff on the resumé. It's true. And they see it as a white thing. Kids still identify this is a white thing, this is a Black thing.

The perception existed that being an urban student placed them at a structural advantage, because of policies like affirmative action. Rather than considering the historical context and need for affirmative action in college admission, they perceived that it allowed students of color to relax, not 'stack their resumés,' and take easier courses. Again, it delimited a need to look deeper into the issue of the overrepresentation of students of color in the basic college prep courses or consider the larger systemic implications of racism. This explanation is also hinged on the notion of urban students as lazy, disinterested, and not academically motivated. It missed the complexity of race, equity, and access issues in education. It was truly a disheartening conversation.

However, Mr. Carmichael's story demonstrated how Black families' utilization of urban identity as a strategy for college negotiated the relations of this identity in new and complex ways. They moved within and against the already present representations of urban identity that were constructed for them. Working within the identity resubstantiated the necessity of an urban other and capitalized on the surprise that was always generated by their success. However, their re-appropriation of this cachet on their own terms worked against fixed representations of urban families caught in discourses of cultural disadvantage, as it demonstrated an agency and active engagement not often attributed to them. Parents like Mr. Carmichael were strategic and aware of the politics of identity. Rather than passive, they proved to be savvy identity consumers, well aware of the commodification of urban-ness, and able to exploit this commodification to the advantage of their students. Troubling, though, is the necessity of these families to position themselves as outside the urban discourse in order to put it to work. Mr. Carmichael made it clear that he was not "urban," but it was an identity he momentarily stepped into as a strategy. Therefore, it was not an innocent practice, but rather one that both disrupted taken-for-granted assumptions and still held in play the inextricably linked damaging discourses.

"I Wanted Her to Be of the World": How White Families Negotiated Urban Student Identity

Most white parents I spoke to mentioned unprompted their support for diversity in the high school. They strongly believed in the importance of diversity and equity and had a sense of pride in sending their children to an "urban" school.

Dr. Steele was a well-respected professor from a local university who volunteered to participate in my study after hearing about it through the PTA. Her daughter was a sophomore with plans to enroll in the IB program, which initially attracted them to the school. She spoke at length about how diversity of the student body impacted their decision to choose OMS. Her comments below demonstrate a desire to support diversity and also showcase her progressive politics by enrolling her daughter in a predominantly Black public high school.

> One of the reasons we wanted to stay in the city of Columbus and why we started out with her in a public school is because *we wanted her to be in the world.* It never was a concern to us that she was going to be a minority . . . because *white kids are the minority at OMS* . . . She was enthralled by the fact that in the cafeteria, because she had seen movies about high school, that there weren't tables for the white kids and tables for the Black kids, that everybody seemed to be involved with everybody else. She seemed to

> be enthralled with the mix of styles that people dressed, the sort of gangster style and preppy kids, and everyone seemed to be interacting.

Yet at the end of this response, there is a hidden acknowledgement of the ways in which urban cachet capitalizes on the materiality of the bodies of students of color:

> I said to her, it looks to me, looking around, that you'll be in a 10 percent minority. She's not just a white girl; she's a tiny white girl. She's 4'10" and weighs 90 lbs NOW. She was smaller then. And I said are you going to be uncomfortable? She said it doesn't feel uncomfortable. *She walks around surrounded by these 6-foot tall . . . [Long pause, as if looking for the appropriate word] gigantic kids. She's at home there.*

The negotiations of urban identity by white families like this one signal another productive moment that demonstrates how commitments to diversity and equity are also inescapable of white privilege. The pride this parent experienced from sending her daughter to an urban school "to be of the world" is very much a white privilege. Whereas Mr. Carmichael was careful to make clear that he was not urban and was even critical of his strategic use of the identity, Dr. Steele was proud of her family's investment in urban education, a pride maybe only available to those marked by whiteness as outside the values of Blackness. "Whiteness as property" (Harris, 1995) served as a form of protection from the commodification and objectification experienced by urban students. It did the work of reaffirming the boundaries of white and Black identity, equating whiteness with privilege and Blackness with disadvantage. The willingness of this family to cross the border into a disadvantaged urban school and their political desire to allow their "tiny white girl" to be around "6-foot tall gigantic kids" was also a manifestation of "interest convergence" (Bell, 1980). Their desires for their child to attend a high-achieving school converged with their commitments to diversity and equity, making the decision to attend an under-resourced school with urban students both academically advantageous and personally fulfilling. OMS is not a typical urban school, but families that capitalize on its urban cachet resurrect traditional notions of disadvantage to do so.

Each form of cachet utilized a construction of urban educational identity overburdened by discourses of disadvantage and risk. These negotiations of urban cachet demonstrated how urban students and schools are discursively constructed through cultural assumptions that derive student failure from those discourses. However, looking at how individual families manipulate urban identity to their advantage renders visible the complex logics of this negotiation. These relations of power were productive of multiple effects; however, each advantage required and desired this particular brand of urban educational other to function, and each appropriation of cachet retraced the limits of urban identity in its reproduction.

The next chapter addresses how students at OMS enacted themselves as educational subjects on their own terms. It attempts to reposition them as agents rather than objects in the educational game.

References

Bell, D. A. (1980). *Brown v Board of Education* and the interest convergence dilemma. *Harvard Educational Review, 93*, 518–533.

Harris, C. I. (1995). Whiteness as property. In K. Crenshaw, N. Gotanda, G. Peller, & K. Thomas (Eds.), *Critical Race Theory: The Key Writings That Formed the Movement* (pp. 276–291). New York: The New Press.

MR. HART'S ENGLISH AND HISTORY "SPLIT" CLASS

I feel like I've been gone for a while from this class. The students have been re-arranged. Mr. Hart's allergy to the new white board requires him to wear medical gloves and put all his notes up in the morning before class. Mr. Fisher is yelling out in the hall, "Let's go. Get to your classrooms." A girl got her lip pierced. Students are commenting on how it's swollen.

This class is high energy. Tim is already in trouble for attempting to eat a cupcake. Mr. Hart says he can go to the Principal's office if he keeps it up. There's a stand-off. "Don't eat it," he says over and over, and tells the student not to test his limits. Esther stomps in looking angry. She sits down in a desk next to me, throws her Dora the Explorer backpack to the ground, and puts her head down on the desk. Tim starts eating again, generating more wrath from his teacher. "Can you just teach please," he finally asks, giving up the fight.

The class moves on uneventfully, until Esther begins loudly drumming her long black acrylic nails on her desk. Her hand has been up, but not answered. I'm wondering myself if she wants to participate or interrupt so I understand why Mr. Hart is ignoring her. No notes or cartoon are on her desk, just her nails drumming with increasing speed and volume.

He ignores her. The class discusses FDR and polio, and how the pictures and images did not show him with crutches or a wheel chair. There are questions about the number of days between election and inauguration. The nails start up again, "Can I go to the office?" she blurts out, aggravated and distraught. "It's an emergency," she says in quick anxious words. I hear her say something under her breath about $70. She leaves without an answer. I want to pull her aside and ask her why she didn't go to him at the beginning of class.

There's a quiet rumble through the class, but then the video about the 1920s starts. He prompts them to "pay attention" and think about "why didn't we have a revolution in America? What are the differences between Hoover and FDR?" Then somebody asks out of turn, "Do those shoes make you look taller?" Kids are so observant, and they know how to use it against you.

The movie starts and hands go up. People want to leave. They need tissues. They need to sneeze or cough. They're thirsty; they need to spit out their gum. One girl seems unable to sit still. She's up and down, making weird noises and hooting at odd moments. She looks at me. I try not to look at her wondering if I'm making her uncomfortable or encouraging her. Esther is back, and Mr. Hart quickly asks her out into the hall. She stomps out. I for some reason focus in on her worn and uncharacteristically juvenile backpack. It either speaks to an innocence or a poverty. I wonder what other frustrations she has from home that she brings to school.

A girl behind Tim plays with his braids. Something in the documentary draws their attention in and the disruptions stop. Students stare at the TV. The class finally quiets down, like a baby. They've either given up or become sucked in by the images on the screen.

6

THOSE STUDENTS

In previous chapters, I have looked at how *urban student identity* was negotiated by schooling actors, and how the process of these negotiations was contingent upon historic and social matrices that pose disadvantage and failure as what is given and known about urban students. So entwined, these ongoing processes continuously constitute relations of power and knowledge that foreclose other possibilities for equity and access to education for students. This chapter explores how these discourses translated at the micro level of daily school practice into bounded identities of success and failure at Ohio Magnet School (OMS).

"Those" Students

During the course of my data collection, I found that parents and teachers perceived two kinds of students at OMS. The "successful student" was an academically driven, intrinsically motivated student who decided along with their parents to apply for the lottery. Advanced Placement (AP) and International Baccalaureate (IB) students were put into this category, and most of the parents I spoke with, particularly white parents, described their students as goal oriented and wanting to be at the school.

IB students in particular were characterized as "the elite" and "the most high-achieving group." Some parents who had students in gifted and talented programs felt that their students had been on a fast track to OMS, and that the new selective admission process, or pre-lottery, formalized this fast track by allowing students to apply based on merit. Students that attended certain alternative middle schools with curriculums that aligned with OMS were also perceived to have a leg up, because of the availability of prerequisites. These academically motivated students, the ones who had shown through grades and advanced courses that they 'want it the most,' were the students that parents and school staff felt OMS was intended to educate. When questioned directly, parents and staff recognized that these students were disproportionately white, but again their explanations focused on individual choices of students and colorblind evaluations of this pattern.

Students talked about the successful student in more complex terms. Natasha, a junior, said that these students were the ones "who really want to do something with their life, want to be something with their life, something major," who were "really smart," and "they want to really challenge themselves." But they were also considered elitist. Jamie, a sophomore, told me that these students "think they're better than you," and "they keep talking about it." He said this was just as disruptive as the kids who misbehave in class.

The second type of student at OMS was the student that had been placed at the school by a family member or guardian, but who did not want to be there. These students were the ones participants referred to as 'those students,' and the discourse around 'those' was rather striking. The parents of these students were perceived to have "just dump(ed) their kids off and s(aid), hey, they're at the best school now, you deal with them." These students were referred to as "the usual ding dongs who don't seem to care one way or the other," "freshmores," "troublemakers," and "underperforming kids" who were "taking up space." They were considered not as focused as the successful students, perceived to be disruptive in the classroom, and failing academically.

On a particularly challenging day that seemed to go from bad to worse for Mr. Fisher, he shared with me his frustration with trying to work with these students. The grades demonstrated that the norm in his sophomore humanities classroom was not the academically driven student but the struggling student. His second quarter grades he felt reflected more accurately the academic climate in some classrooms at OMS: 31 Fs, 11 Ds, 8 Cs, 3 Bs, and 0 As. The highest score in his class was an 82 percent. Two students who had not missed a day of school had unbelievably low grades. One white boy had a 7 percent average and another African American boy had an 8 percent. Of the 31 Fs, 23 were African American students (14 male and 9 female), and the remaining 8 were white, and he believed that most of these students had struggled in 9th grade humanities as well. He speculated that based on his interactions with parents that most of these students came from single-parent, female-headed households who were financially stressed. He also felt that these same kids were the ones that parents had "turned over to us" hoping that the school could turn them around.

These students and the stresses they brought to the school were talked about as "the burdens." Mr. Hart explained that OMS had created a focused academic environment:

> [a]gainst the odds . . . Over the last few years the burdens on the teaching staff and the school have grown. The burdens of the social problems

> coming into the school have increased, not beyond control, but they've increased. So we've had a lot of students who just aren't academic.

In the past, students who were unsuccessful at OMS could transfer back to their own high school, but the option for students to complete credit recovery for failing classes had made it practically unnecessary for them to exit and made it difficult for the school to direct them into other programs. OMS found itself in a new position of having "to deal with (our) share of the burdens too." They also noticed that they were getting more students who were not as prepared as they had been in the past, and they attributed this to a greater proportion of students and/or parents choosing OMS, because it was one of the safest high schools in the district, not because of its academic focus.

Teachers and staff felt stretched in terms of time and resources to serve students in a social service capacity. As a guidance counselor explained, "I can't be a full-time counselor for kids experiencing problems, although that's what they train me to do in college. You don't have enough time to do that." She went on to tell me about these other issues that included homelessness, transience, pregnancy, and anger management. Teachers I interviewed also speculated about violence, drug addiction in the home, and poverty.

Students also agreed that there were "those students" that "sleep," "argue with teachers," "act out," "yell and cuss and scream a lot," and are "the loud fighting type." Jamie confirmed "there's two types of students at OMS: there are the people that are passionate about their social life and people that are passionate about their educational life." There were students in some of the basic college prep classes I observed that displayed this kind of behavior. Other students felt that these students had a negative impact on the learning environment.

When I asked students to describe what was meant when references were made to "those" students, their descriptions took on racial and socioeconomic contexts associated with urban identity. During a focus group, Michael stated that he felt those students were not just the Black kids, but a diverse group of students. Isabella, an African American girl who had attended the language immersion school disagreed: "Most of the people who do act like that, it might be their environment that they live in, because I don't think anybody that lives where he [Michael] lives would act like that." Michael was a white student from the predominantly white middle class neighborhood north of the school. Later he went on to speculate that, "Statistically with the demographics of where people live and the work ethics associated with *that race* stereotypically might (have) some impact on it." Though he did not refer specifically to Black students, it was clear that this was the demographic to which he was referring when he talked about "that race."

Natasha's talk about "those students" was also heavily invested with racialized urban discourses that associate Black students with failure and lack of interest in school:

> *I just believe, not trying to be racist, I'm partially Black. I just believe that, oh this sounds so bad. Black people are really lazy.* They don't like to really apply themselves, because they figure what's there after high school. What is there for me to do? *Because there are so many stereotypes against Black people nowadays where they can't succeed when they do this, they can't succeed when they do that . . .*
>
> I know if I had a choice now I would have been in AP or IB looking back at it. But the IB students and AP students are really students who really want to do something with their life, want to be something with their life, something major. *And I already know that most of the Black students here aren't really into that.* They really don't care whether or not they get really good grades or if they get something on their transcript like that. They're not really worried about it. They're just worried about what they're wearing tomorrow.
>
> I know for a fact that certain people here, like the Black students that are taking AP or IB, they're really smart . . . It doesn't have to be everybody in there. I think it's a good mixture because you don't want a lot of . . . *I won't say you don't want a lot of Blacks and whites together, but its always predominantly a white thing, because we're the minority group, so of course the majority group is going to take over.* And they don't want to sit in regular classes and have regular studies. They want to really challenge themselves.

"Those students" was a local representation of the urban student at OMS. Discursive constructions of "those students" were raced in specific ways. These discourses had strong implications for how teachers and parents saw students and how students saw themselves as agents in their own education. Natasha's understanding of herself and other students of color was both troubling and complex. Though she constructed Black students as "lazy," she followed this with a commentary on the material experiences of discrimination that students face after high school in terms of jobs and higher education. However, the discourses that hold sway in her discussion are those heavy with stereotypes of Black students as apathetic and disinterested.

It is also clear from discussions above, just as discursive constructions of "those students" were overburdened by Blackness, discourses of success were equally "colored" by whiteness. Successful students were perceived to be white, but also it bore out that white students had more access to the academic markers of success—IB and AP courses. The circulation of these discourses and representations had material implications for daily lives of students and how they saw themselves as educational agents.

In the next section I want to demonstrate how whiteness, often viewed as an invisible marker of race, "colored" the fight for the selective admission policy and how the discursively racialized identities of the "successful student" and "those students" were put into play.

The Fight for Selective Admission

The selective admission policy, also referred to as the pre-lottery, was a request made by parents for years that the district rejected for different reasons. Selective admission was conceived to allow students to apply to OMS ahead of the regular lottery and be competitively selected for 1 of 50 seats based on merit rather than luck of the draw. The number of regular lottery seats at OMS was to be reduced to 100 to maintain the small school climate. But rather than open up a selective admission to appease what was perceived as a small but loud constituency of white parents, the district increased the number of regular lottery seats to improve access for more students. The Columbus City Schools (CCS) district was concerned with equity at OMS, and this was viewed as at odds with the parents' and school's concerns with protecting its excellence. Race worked at the seams of this relationship, and I argue it is this tension between equity and excellence that "colored" the relationship between the predominantly white PTA at OMS and district administration. Perceptions of elitism were intricately tied to the whiteness of the PTA parents and informed the direct accusations of racism against the PTA by the district.

Though in most conversations with parents racial issues at the school were read through discourses of individual student responsibility and colorblindness, issues of race were acknowledged in discussions of the PTA's long fight for the pre-lottery, which was finally approved by the district for the 2008–2009 school year. Their whiteness "colored" the pre-lottery, their fight with the district, and potentially the bodies that gained admission through the program. The pre-lottery was deeply tied to racialized discursive constructions of "those students" and "successful students." The practices of white parents advocating for their students took shape within always already circulating white privilege. Moving forward here, I read these practices through power/knowledge relations that racialize parental advocacy and student access to schools to look at how whiteness "colored" the pre-lottery.

A white parent of two girls at the school, who was a member of the district task force that created the pre-lottery, explained she was motivated by the inability of the district to serve all of its high-achieving students with challenging enrichment opportunities:

> I think one of my big things was, "(We) know you worked really hard. Congratulations! You can go to a mediocre school." Or a school that doesn't have as many course offerings or advanced placement offerings. That just doesn't make sense to me.

But she also discussed how "not everyone wants to go there for the right reason . . . and they really don't want to do the work (and) *they're taking the seat from somebody else who might really want to go there and work really hard.*"

Though they were often talked about in de-raced terms, it was "those students" who were attending OMS for the "wrong reasons" that also drove desires for the pre-lottery.

Parents often talked nostalgically about OMS in the past and hesitantly about how they perceived the school had changed, and not for the better. The nostalgia was tied to being more populated in the past by the "successful students," while the changes at OMS were mostly attributed to the burdens and disruptions the school had taken on with the increase in "those students" coming to the school for other than academic reasons.

As one white mother of an OMS graduate and a current student stated during a focus group, "part of why we tried to do the pre-lottery (was) to get more kids that really wanted to learn and that were focused on academics and try to bring it back to the way OMS used to be." Another parent was critical of the pre-lottery and believed that parents had driven the issue, because OMS was "getting underperforming kids":

> I have friends in other schools that are teachers, and there are some concerns about how we got to get the cream of the crop in our lottery—pick out 50. And I'm not quite sure how we got that legally. I think the parents drove that. I think it was because we were getting underperforming kids.

If we read the desires for a pre-lottery through racialized discourses of urban student identity that produce "those students" as Black and "successful students" as predominantly white, the pre-lottery issue is "colored" by these power/knowledge frameworks. Parents inescapably worked within this grid, and purposely or not, their advocacy for their children adversely affected "those students." The color, the whiteness, of the parents advocating for the pre-lottery produced racial tensions with the district, making whiteness visible:

> This is my seventh year in the school, and we talked about this for years. It really fell on deaf ears with the administration. Two years ago our PTA president started a dialogue directly with the superintendant, but what I think really gave us a leg up is that with the new Gardener Middle School, if you were lucky enough to lottery in there you were guaranteed a spot at (another school) because you were prepared in the arts . . . I had quite a heated debate with the former principal about this, but she just didn't want to listen. But it was a lot of persistence I think, because we have this really great rigorous program, why shouldn't it serve the kids that want it most? And all we said was "why can't we offer a portion of our seats to kids who demonstrate?" They wouldn't have to be lucky enough to lottery in . . . Why aren't there other programs like this in the district where kids can be, where they get what they need, not just based on random lottery? And it was difficult. We argued for years. *The first time we talked to*

the superintendent, unfortunately the group was all white, so she basically said we were elitists, and we didn't want Black kids in the school.

Teachers too recognized that a tension existed in the lottery between "those students" that got a seat at OMS and "successful students" who lost a seat to the academically unmotivated. The district long ignored requests and demands for a pre-lottery, but then suddenly they changed their tune. Some speculated that it was because the increased enrollment hurt the program and caused the district to give in. Others believed that it was the increase in "those students" that led to the implementation of the pre-lottery:

> [i]f you had told me they were going to do that I would have said "you are crazy," because they dug their heels in for years. I've been here 27 years, and we started talking about the need for that thing when I'd been here 2 years . . .
>
> Because there were people here that were not fitting . . . We would pick 150, and 50 or 25 of them would be like "Weeee! Wooooo!" So it rankled people. *There are kids out there who would really give their eye teeth to be in this program, and you're just sitting there taking up a spot.* So there's where it came from, and the district would hear nothing. They would not even entertain the discussion. Just like, get out, close the door, don't, no, stop. Then suddenly . . . We were beginning to have trouble with an imbalance of kids, too many kids, that . . . There's certainly got to be a critical mass of kids that want to do this or . . . I mean you can take them to water.

This teacher perceived the district approved the pre-lottery to help OMS recover from the increase in enrollment and attempt to re-balance the population with "successful students." For parents and teachers, race was perceived to be inconsequential to their desires for a pre-lottery. They were interested in providing enrichment to "successful students" and shifting the balance back to an academically motivated climate. Though many wanted to ignore the role that race played in their negotiations, it proved to be inescapable. Whiteness colored desires for the pre-lottery.

Conclusion

I had no way of knowing whether or not the 50 pre-lottery students were predominantly white or what the demographic breakdown was of the group. Several teachers at the school told me that they did not want to find out whom the pre-lottery students were so that they could verify that it was improving the academic climate as intended. Some however openly worried that the selective admission did privilege white students:

> The peculiar and depressing and disturbing part of this is my daughter is on the school bus that goes through Clintonville. Last year that bus was practically empty; this year there is no room to sit. Most of those, all freshmen. So this is what's worrisome. Most of those freshman who got in that pre-application pre-lottery program are white, middle-class kids from Clintonville. And that's the part that's of concern.

Students needed better educational resources at their middle schools in order to access the pre-lottery. This school bus route might very well be a direct indicator of how selective admission favored white students. Recalling Chapter 3, practices of racialized enrollments into AP and IB courses were entangled with structural issues like the type of middle school attended, student awareness of and access to prerequisites, and the availability of parents or teachers to advocate for the student. The pre-lottery was equally bound up with the same structural inequalities along lines of race and class. They placed students at a disadvantage when it came to accessing opportunities, like a selective admission seat in a high-achieving school.

The pre-lottery was justified in and through de-raced notions of "those" students. Though parents desired to de-race the fight for the pre-lottery, white privilege circulated in powerful ways, becoming entangled with racialized discourses of urban student identity that allowed the district to overlook the structural issues that might impact a student's eligibility to apply. White parents read their own intentions as de-raced and about general access to better educational resources. However, their increased ability to advocate for their students functioned as a site of power/knowledge where whiteness "colored" the pre-lottery and contained urban students within fixed discourses of disadvantage, disinterest, and risk.

When a white female student told me, "the district is all about political correctness," it was not expressed in a positive way. She felt that the desperate attempts to provide "equal opportunities for everybody" avoided discussion of the fact that some programs "were better than others" and some students were "better prepared for the future." Even this 14-year-old freshman voiced tensions between equity and excellence, and perceived them to be irreconcilable. I am hoping for another frame, one that sees excellence as impossible without equity. How might we move to disrupt these tendencies to situate urban students within discourses of disadvantage and deprivation, and instead see them on their own terms, opening up the possibilities for access and achievement in public schools? In the next chapter, teachers and students show us another way to think and do that disrupts the fixing of identity to shift to an *unfixing* of the urban subject, one that is open to the messiness and complications produced when students are seen as agents of education on their own terms.

"HE JUST GAVE US ALL THE ANSWERS"

Boys' Participation in 10th Grade Humanities

I moved to an empty chair at the back of the room behind a group of boys. It's a very good spot, particularly to listen to their whisperings and exchanges. A white boy with dirty, slightly greasy, brown hair sits to my left. I saw him my first day here, sitting alone out on the back pavement at lunch. I remember his shoes, black airwalks with bright green laces. He's got the same shoes on, a pair of loose tan cargo pants worn out at the bottom from dragging under his sneakers, and a dingy gray jacket. His nails are dirty. He's got nothing out on his desk, just a small red drawstring backpack next to him on the floor. He looks disinterested.

Today the students are turning in their final essays with the works cited page, rough draft, and pre-writing attached. Mrs. Perry provides very complicated instructions for ordering and stapling the assignments together, and I can barely follow her. She and Mr. Fisher hand out multiple staplers. Hands go up and students begin asking her to repeat the instructions.

An announcement comes over the loud speaker. Dr. Davis asks that if anyone has found a purple wallet with a green frog on it to please return it to the office for a reward. That must be Esther's wallet and the reason for her outburst in Mr. Hart's class last period.

There's quiet talk amongst the students as they staple and pass in their work. The African American male in front of the boy with the airwalks asks him for his paper. He shakes his head and says unapologetically, "I didn't read the book." The young man in front of him replies, "Well, I wrote something," with a look of surprise on his face that the boy didn't do anything but even he did. He continues to get chided by others around him, "you could have wrote something" another boy says. While this discussion is going on, another Black student in front of me passes a computer printout of high top sneakers to his friend on my right.

Mr. Fisher is his usual joking self. After he moves a student to the front row, he asks for the class to get out a worksheet on the Industrial Revolution that they were to complete for homework. The white boy beside me has nothing to turn in and the boy in front of him can't find his. He reluctantly combs through a folder filled with various wrinkled and smudged worksheets from multiple classes. I don't think he really cares if he finds it.

I quickly take a head count while the class is reviewing the answers. Students are paying attention, and those that are not are quiet. The white boy next to me stares listlessly at his desk and around the room. The student in front of him who could never find his worksheet is doodling to pass the time. I can see pages and pages of faces and crosses as he flips through his notebook.

Count:
White females 5
White males 2
African American females 20
African American males 18
Asian American 1

The worksheet they've just gone over gets passed up for a grade. The doodling student says to the slacker, "He just gave us all the answers," again shocked at his classmate's lack of effort.

The next assignment discussed is a propaganda poster that they have to make. The doodler turns around to ask the slacking white boy if he's even going to do one. He shrugs. He's busy folding a note he just wrote.

Mr. Fisher discusses the importance of accuracy and reminds students to check their history and use the internet. One African American girl asks, "Why can't it be pretty? Why does it have to be all serious?" He responds with his usual sarcasm and humor, "Pictures of flowers and ponies provoke me to violence."

All the while Mrs. Perry is at the board making notes. I notice that her hair has fallen, her red suit jacket is disheveled, and her make-up has expired. It's been a long Friday.

She begins her part of the lecture on All Quiet on the Western Front, *and Mr. Fisher leaves. "Really try to remember to bring your books to class," she says. Some kids don't even bother to look for a book, while others have it out and I can see their highlights.*

I enjoy sitting in these classes. I think about all the lectures I zoned out on and things I probably missed. They are reading from a handout. A boy at the front reads like my partner, in fits and starts, mispronouncing words. People laugh, but he continues unfazed. Mrs. Perry supports him to continue and she smiles as he reads. I have seen so clearly the level of compassion and support students get from their teachers, which is one of the reasons why teachers like Mr. Fisher are so popular and well liked by the students.

People have their highlighters out unprompted. "Let's highlight that paragraph please," she says. She asks a very broad question "Is war senseless" and there is a brief discussion. Her comments are slanted and liberal, but I don't mind. I'm glad. The bright blonde with braces makes a comment that's more conservative than I would have expected. This class works. It's large and full of mixed ability students, but the teachers manage to keep it together.

My eyes roam the room to count five boys not taking notes. An African American male two seats to my right is looking at a worksheet, held so close to his face it's almost touching his nose. His nails are bitten to the quick, bright red and faintly bloody . . .

7

ON THEIR OWN TERMS

In spite of the issues of stratified enrollment and the pre-lottery, teachers and staff also felt strongly that "we take all kids in through the lottery . . . and we eventually do good things with most kids." Though Ohio Magnet School (OMS) had a reputation for producing elite students and "skimming off the top" the best students in the district, it was very clear during my time there that they were educating a full spectrum of students from the very driven to the very apathetic and everything in between. It is the students that did not fit neatly into either category of the "successful student" or "those students," the ones that exceeded what were perceived to be the knowable properties of their existence, that made clear that all students are subjects in the making, remaking, and resistance of identity. They are urban educational subjects on their own terms.

These students were "elusive" (Yon, 2000) and fluid agents in refashioning urban educational identity, and it was an on-going process of becoming. I refer to the students as elusive agents to signal a conceptualization of them as subjects in the making, remaking, and resisting of identity that elude any fixed form of representation. Subjectivity, the product and process of lived experience, is discursively situated within the grid of power and knowledge, but permeable to the complicated ways students live their lives.

Rather than asserting that I can truly know the urban subject, I assert the necessary failure of ethnography, and I recognize that subjects produce themselves in ways that exceed what is given and known. This slipping and sliding, this failure to fix, makes use of the disruptions and irreconcilable moments to trouble taken-for-granted understandings of urban students and make room for other possibilities. How is "success" operationalized, resisted, and reconstructed at OMS through students' practices of schooling, and how do these practices provide an understanding of urban student subjectivity in relation to macro and micro policies and practices that construct urban student identity?

There is an inherent complicity within social science research to continually resurrect the *urban other*. There is also the equally damaging possibility of delegitimizing the lived experiences of systemic poverty and oppression that do indeed impact students in urban schools. The writing here inhabits the tension of how to both legitimate the materiality of urban schooling for students and teachers without, as Fine (1995) so adeptly states, "containing and displaying" them.

There is potential to reconceive this tension, fight the tendencies of containment and for display, by constantly troubling the representations that get produced and looking for possibilities, openings, and leaks in the limits of our understanding. Students at OMS are highly recognized for their academic achievement. At this school, race, poverty, and other urban "disadvantages" are articulated with academic success. Rather than being perceived as students who have been transformed by outside forces, how might they be reconsidered as aspirational, dedicated, and committed? How might all students succeed if they were afforded the opportunity of this school?

The following portraits attempt to look at urban students on their own terms, admitting that these terms are elusive, and that their negotiations slide both in and out of the traditional discourses of urban identity. But it is in the slippage that urban subjectivity becomes unfixed from taken-for-granted notions about the larger dominant discourses of disadvantage and risk, as well as the local discursive constructions of "those students" that are entangled with urban and racialized subtexts. The ways in which these students inhabit, re-appropriate, and puncture the containment of urban identity show the unboundedness of their becoming, replete with (im)possible understandings of how these students negotiate academic success and achievement on their own terms.

Natasha

> *I sit in Mr. Fisher's room and wait for my interviewee to show up to first block study hall. She arrives just after the bell. She has an attitude with him, and he has one with her. He asks her to come to his desk, but she doesn't seem to hear him. He waves her over in an exaggerated manner, rolling his eyes. He mutters under his breath about "these kids" and tells her I'm here. There's some back talk on her part, and her tough demeanor makes me worry about how this interview is going to go, if she really wants to participate. I get the impression that she's a difficult student. But then we leave and I meet someone different.*
>
> *Natasha is tall, maybe 5'9", and thin. She is in Mr. Fisher's afternoon split class. I learn during the course of our interview that she identifies as African American and Puerto Rican. She's dressed comfortably in jeans, sneakers, and a jacket with her hair pulled up into a high ponytail. I introduce myself as we head down the quiet hallway to the cafeteria with a box of fresh glazed donuts. She immediately*

> *begins asking me questions about going to college, and her enthusiasm catches me off guard after the interchange I saw between her and her teacher. She's smiling and lit up in a way I never expected, and the furrowed brows and vinegary disposition I witnessed have dissipated. She asks me what my degree will be when I graduate. "How do you get a PhD?" "How long does it take?" She tells me eagerly, cutting me off before I can finish, that she plans to attend a four-year college to get her bachelors, but eventually wants to get "the highest degree" she can get, which for her is an MBA. She has chosen a university, is preparing to take her SATs, and is saving money for college. She wants to go into business and fashion design. She takes a fresh glazed donut from the box once we get seated in the cafeteria, and we get started with our interview.*
>
> *She works to support herself and her mother, has younger siblings, and is trying to save for a car. She's very conscientious about money. Kmart works her close to 40 hours a week. She gets home late and usually does homework at school during study hall and steals time during class. She recognizes that her B average grades would be better if she didn't work, but I can see that in a lot of ways she doesn't have a choice. I am really glad to have her in my study. She is the typical OMS student, but not the one in the spotlight. She's the student that they capitalize on when they want to be urban.*

Natasha inhabited a space of difference that defied her containment precisely within the discourses of "those students" or the "successful student." Natasha failed to fit within binary formulations that would make her simply one of "those students," and she shifted my gaze to recognize the absence of the complexities of their lives when urban students are imagined. Her subjectivity, her lived negotiations at the intersection of discourse, power, and knowledge transgressed imposed boundaries or categorizations.

Early on in the interview, she cast herself simultaneously as both a student looking for a challenge and a student who was academically disinterested. She, and not a parent or guardian, took the initiative to enter the lottery for OMS:

> You know most children here say that their parent picked it for them. Well me and my mom sat down and talked about it. I would rather go to a school where its one of the top ranking schools in Columbus . . . so that's why I chose to go here. Right when they were telling us about the lottery and they showed us all the names, and I was like, I've never heard of that before and that would be interesting to go to a place you never heard of and no one's ever been there. Especially in my family I know I'm the first one to go here . . . It wasn't my mom's decision.

However, she also referred to herself as "lazy" several times during the interview. She told me, "I have really horrible study habits, and I'm lazy as I don't know what," and this laziness was often asserted as a reason for her average grades and inability to complete her homework, "I got a high B in that class and I barely still didn't do anything. I don't know why I'm so lazy with that kind of stuff. I just don't feel like doing it." The discourse of individual choice permeated her explanation of homework habits and grades, and this choice was tinged with racialized conceptualizations of herself as lazy, academically disinterested, and unmotivated—characteristics inscribed onto the bodies of "those students" at OMS.

It was quite obvious though that her family struggled financially, and Natasha took it upon herself to support her mother and her siblings while also trying to save money and meet her own needs:

Sara: Do you wish you didn't have to work so much after school?

Natasha: I wish that a lot. Like yesterday I didn't go to work even though I was supposed to, just because it takes a lot out of you and it wears you out. You get home and you're seriously tired, because it's basically like you go to school from like 8 and you come home at 10:30 at night. And you only get like 20 minutes to be at home and eat and all that kind of stuff. I think that if I didn't have to work so much I would be happy. But then again when you see the paychecks that you get your kind of OK it was worth it.

Sara: What do you spend your money on?

Natasha: I'm saving it for my car. My mom kind of gets mad, because I'll pay my phone bill. My mom doesn't pay my phone bill. You know most students have their parents pay for it. I pay my phone bill, and anything I want I get for myself. I don't ask my mom for anything. I save up for my car. I put $150 down every paycheck. Give it to my mom. I want her to hold the money, because I think I'll spend it if I had it by myself. She kind of gets mad because I spend my money on clothes sometimes. She's like "you have a lot of clothes don't spend your money on it." I don't know; I love clothes. I just love things that you don't have that you weren't able to afford before.

My mom did have to do this all by herself, having four kids and having a job all by herself, having to pay a mortgage, and having to pay a car, and all this stuff by herself . . .

She kind of gets annoyed. She'll be like "well Natasha I have to get this and that." This might sound selfish, but I hate when people complain about it. I mean I don't hate when she complains, because you know I know she means for the good. If she could get it for me she would. I just can't stand the complaining. I'm like, "I might just get a job and get it for myself. You won't have to complain and worry about it."

The only thing she does for me is pick me up from work every single night before she goes to work. So I know if I have a car she won't even have to worry about that. I can just take myself and bring myself back home, and she'll be all on her own doing whatever she does.

Sara: Do you buy your own food?

Natasha: Umm, hmm. I give her $100 every time I get paid. My mom will sit there and be like "you all eat all the food all the time." So I just give her money so she'll have more money to add on to what she usually buys, and she won't have to worry about the food being gone in two days.

As a student, Natasha inhabited this tension between family responsibilities and academic opportunities. The "choices" she made about her courses took place within a network of structural disadvantages entangled with racialized discourses about "those" students.

Sara: If you could work less what would you do?

Natasha: If I could work (less) I would study more. It would make life so much easier than having to come to school and start doing work and worrying about "am I doing this right or what's going all wrong."

Sara: Do they know you work?

Natasha: They don't know that. Most of them don't know that I work. Mr. Fisher knows that I work, but I still manage a B in his class. I go to their class and they're like "why are you so tired and why are you half asleep." So I'm just like "I have a job." It's kind of hard to keep up with all this stuff. I'm doing your work at night and trying to sleep. It's really hard. If I didn't have a job as much working I would do a lot better.

Sara: Do you think they think you're a serious student?

Natasha: When I apply my mind I'm really serious about it.

Though she could easily be read as an average college preparatory student who enrolled in basic courses, slept in class, and struggled to complete her homework, she continued to hold on to an educational identity that was academically invested and headed for college. She spoke about her love of science and how it came "easy" to her, and she was enthusiastic and definite about her college plans and career goals. Natasha was an educational subject on her own terms, one who negotiated family struggles with academic expectations. Though her academic efforts might have been read as average, she proved to be a savvy self-advocate independently entering the lottery and making educational decisions to increase her opportunities. If we read against the racialized discourses that construct her as "lazy" and disinterested, we find a subject who re-appropriates high achievement on her own terms, taking advantage of educational opportunities, while managing adult responsibilities against academic expectations made for traditional students from structurally advantaged households.

Esther

Esther was a student in Mr. Hart's afternoon split. She was a junior, and I overheard her say in conversations that she had not passed her OGT for the second year in a row. She had long straight hair that she dyed often—jet black, flaming red, golden brown. She came to school in t-shirts, hoodies, and jeans, her shoes worn, and she carried a weathered Dora the Explorer backpack. Her appearance stood out in contrast with the other girls she tried to fit in with or converse with in class, who insisted on new clothes and shoes and talked about shopping.

If there was any student that most represented one of "those students," it was Esther. I observed her in Mr. Hart's class on numerous occasions, and in reviewing my field notes, there is not a day of observations that went by without some type of disruption from her, and most of the time these disruptions were severe and resulted in her being asked to leave. The following is an example of an average day in class with Esther:

> *Esther is trying to answer questions in class, but is also making comments to the students who are handing out hall passes for sports pictures . . . Mr. Hart is trying to lecture over this interruption. He tells them to highlight the date on the* New York Times *article and explains that it is a primary source document. They all start working on the assignment while he returns tests . . .*
>
> *As students get the tests back, I try to steal glances at their scores. I see 80s, 50s and 70 percents. Esther looks at her test and has no problem airing her grade, "36 percent, oh my God. Oh Jesus. Did you grade my other worksheet?"*
>
> . . .
>
> *Everybody is awake, taking notes, and paying attention. There is very little noise or disruption at the moment. Esther takes off her sports t-shirt with a smug grin and sits at her desk for a few moments in a tank top—against dress code. She pulls a regular shirt out of her backpack and slips it on cutting glances at students around her. As Mr. Hart is directing the class to "write it down" and makes comparisons between the lesson and the current situation with Iraq and Afghanistan, Esther sprays perfume into the air and lets it float down over her. She holds the bottle up to Tim's nose. "Put that away," Mr. Hart orders. "I am!" He shifts back to the class, "Guys I need you to focus." Suddenly Esther shouts, "You rude man dang!" I can't figure out why, but then she says that he didn't see her hand up, and that she has to go to the bathroom. Because of her outburst, he tells her to leave the class, take herself to the bathroom and then to the office, but she comes back . . .*
>
> *Kids are talking again . . . Students are complaining that Mr. Hart didn't get their homework graded. He hands it back so they can study for a test. Esther accuses him of throwing the worksheet at her, "That's disrespectful," she says with a great deal of hostility. The class is getting ready to go to the computer lab. "You can walk with me," he tells her. She says "No" and stomps out the door ahead of him.*

But then there were instances when she participated in class that demonstrated preparation and engagement. Her participation had a positive effect on the classroom:

> *The class is reading* Being There *by Jerzy Kosinski, and they are unbelievably engaged with the text in spite of the fact that several of them admit they haven't started reading it. Mr. Hart spends the majority of the period leading students through an introduction to the story. Not much has changed in this classroom since my last visit. Melinda still gets up several times to blow her nose out in the hall. Mr. Hart is still prompting them to "write it down," and there is still quite a bit of noise, personal conversations, and unnecessary outbursts that he continues to ignore. If he stopped for all the interruptions, he would never get any teaching done.*
>
> *Different from other visits is how they are very engaged. They love talking about the story to the point where there are voices on top of voices, and it takes some finesse for Mr. Hart to wrangle in the conversations. Esther surprises me. She's read the book. She answers questions and refers to specific pages for examples. She still exhibits attention-seeking behaviors, yells, and has side conversations, but she's also participating. There also seems to be a renewed teacher-student relationship between her and Mr. Hart:*
>
> | | |
> |---|---|
> | Esther (standing up): | *Can I get some water . . . by chance? (The character in the book is named Chance.)* |
> | Mr. Hart: | *That's what lunch is for . . . by chance.* |
> | Esther: | *I don't have $ . . . you owe me $2 by chance.* |
> | Mr. Hart: | *I do owe you $2 by chance . . .* |
>
> *They are both smiling, and they're exchange provokes laughter from the class.*

When I asked Mr. Hart about Esther, he resisted classifying her as one of "those students." He perceived that she wanted to be at OMS, because she recognized the opportunity it provided for her to escape the climate of her home school:

> A lot of immaturity. But when it comes down to it she does a decent amount of the work. She got a C in my class. She didn't do it all, but she did enough. So why is she still here? I think even students that don't like every aspect of [this school] recognize that there is value in it somehow. But it's also a very safe place for them to be . . . Even the kids that are like Esther, that sort of have an attitude that don't seem to want to be here. Ask them to go to their home school. There's a social aspect of not wanting to be here, but then there is a private aspect of wanting to be here. They may push the rules, test the waters; they would not go back to their home school. If they test the waters [at the home school] there's going to be other consequences . . . because they live in those neighborhoods.

He saw her as both disruptive and simultaneously "committed" to her education and empowered by being there, something I only glimpsed during my observations:

Mr. Hart: She's not that bad . . . She answers back . . . She doesn't have any control. She's very self-centered at this moment in her life. It's very simple; if you challenge her she challenges you back. She probably does that to her mother.

Sara: The day she lost her wallet . . . she was strumming her nails so loud . . .

Mr. Hart: She's gonna walk out. If they walk out I have to write them up, but I don't always do that. That's the thing . . . *but overall she's a committed student. But there are other people with behavior problems who aren't committed students.*

Sara: You have a different picture of her because you know her grades . . . She's definitely a presence in the classroom, where there are some kids, I almost don't even know they're here.

Mr. Hart: I think we'll solve the problems of education when we learn to deal with kids on a more individual basis. *I think what frustrates me about teaching is you feel you're perpetuating a system that is not empowering its students. It can be. This school is empowering to a lot of people.*

I tried throughout the year to interview Esther. Finally, in late May, I tracked her down in the hall and asked if she would meet with me at lunch. She was flattered, "You want to talk to me?" I came in the following week to find out that she had been expelled for the last few days of the year and the first day of the next year for letting off smoke bombs in the hallway with two other students.

Esther was an elusive subject. She slipped in and out of discourses of urban identity and the "those students" category. Her disruptive behavior signaled this location, but Mr. Hart read her differently, with a sense of empathy and compassion that I found admirable, and this allowed him, and me, to see her as a student on her own terms. There were those moments when she was invested, on task, and making a contribution to the classroom. As he stated at the end of our interview, he did not want to perpetuate an education system that failed to empower its students. I witnessed from Mr. Hart, though he was often confronted with talking and disrespectful behavior, a desire for students to be empowered by OMS on their own terms, and he tried to meet them halfway to help them do this.

Ryan

Ryan was in Mr. Fisher's 12th grade Advanced Placement (AP) English class. His quiet demeanor stood in contrast to his tall, football-like stature. He was white with shoulder-length dirty blonde hair. He wore baggy clothes and sometimes wrapped a long flowing scarf around his neck, and his style set him apart from the other students. He had a girlfriend who was also in the class, but I would not have known of their relationship unless he had told me, as they rarely acknowledged each other in the classroom and looked more like friends in the hallways. She was planning to attend a university a few hours away, while Ryan planned to enroll in community college to save money.

He sat quietly in the front row, usually watching and listening, flipping through the reading material. He participated only as needed, maybe once or twice per class session, but his comments were thoughtful. From time to time, he would say hi to me in the hall or share some random information with me before class. In a few moments time I learned a lot about him:

> *As I head into the classroom I make eye contact with Ryan in the hall. I ask if there is a test or quiz, and he says that they are going downtown to see* A Midsummer Night's Dream *at the Southern Theater. He seems excited. He tells me that he doesn't have a car and has never been downtown before. I comment quickly that he'll definitely enjoy the Southern; it's my favorite theater in town. I take my usual seat, a chair in the closet doorway, and wonder how a kid in Columbus could manage to never go downtown—just a few miles away. So he's never been to the mall, the museum, the library?*

The first time we arranged to meet after school for an interview he stood me up. He eventually called to apologize, and we rescheduled—he had forgotten. The next time we met, he had gotten a haircut, and it was a stunning change. The Principal walked into the conference room where we were meeting and jokingly called him "lover boy," teasing him about his new look. He smiled shyly. While he drank hot chocolate and ate a brownie I bought him, the shyness dissipated, and I learned that Ryan was highly intelligent and full of opinion, but made little effort in school. He lived alone, worked part-time at a local restaurant, and rode his bike as much as possible so as to avoid public transportation. He wanted to be a veterinarian.

Though Ryan was in the AP class, he situated himself within and against the discursive construction of the elite, successful students:

> I've always been a brainiac, since middle school, but I was always bored, so I never tried. I was suspended from kindergarten because I told the teacher her class was boring. It happened here too. I don't get good grades—the occasional B, but I average Cs and Ds. They wanted to test me for gifted, but I refused to take it. What's the difference? It's just the same stuff I already know. AP English is the first AP class I've taken all four years. I find it more tedious than challenging. I don't think OMS is a more challenging high school . . . Once I get into college it will actually matter.

He saw himself as different from the other students in his AP class, and said that most of his school acquaintances were in "regular" classes:

> Nobody knows me outside of school. Outside of school I'm completely different. I don't want to hang out with anyone here [with the exception of his girlfriend and a few friends] . . . I'm an outcast anywhere else. I'm a hermit. Anywhere else they say "stay away from us," but not here.

He was gifted, but admittedly academically unmotivated. He was not disruptive, but he was not making the most of his opportunity at OMS. He told me, "not everyone likes to go here . . . school's a boring place." Ryan's academic behaviors closely associate him with "those students" who took up space, but he situated himself outside of this discourse as well:

Sara: So who are "those" students?

Ryan: They are loud, obnoxious . . . they have no respect. They're always texting, they don't pay attention. I'm not a model student, but I give them [the teachers] respect. They [other students] don't do anything. I don't try, but I do the work.

Ryan gave little consideration to the other issues going on in his life—factors that I thought equally contributed to a lack of interest in school:

> I live by myself. I'm comfortable alone. My mom lives with her new husband in [a town outside of Columbus]. I buy my own clothes, but my mom comes every weekend to check up on me and bring me food. I share a house with my brother. He works from 5:00 am to 3:00 pm.

His father lived out of state, and they had very little contact. In another portion of the interview he mentioned that he had an older sister who was found in a crack house about ten years ago, not far from where I had lived on the east side of Columbus.

Like Natasha and other students I interviewed who held jobs and struggled with life outside of school, Ryan failed to consider the impact of this on his academic experiences. He spoke of his disinterest as a choice or coincidence, something that resulted because he did not think high school was important. In college he would choose to do better because "it will actually matter."

He held onto his college aspirations. Regardless of perceived lack of investment in high school, college was a given for Ryan, just as it was for the majority of students at OMS. Therefore, while structural inequalities shaped his experience as an "urban" student who had never made it downtown, his negotiations provided another example of how students at OMS became educational subjects on their own terms. Dominant discourses failed to capture the indeterminancy of Ryan's subjectivity or the materiality of his lived experiences.

In early fall of 2009, I ran into Ryan while he was at work. My family and I frequented his restaurant, because it was loud and kid-friendly. He stopped by my table, and I asked him how college was going, hoping to get a good report. He expressed that he was struggling to pay for it, and struggling to make it to work and to class. He had to increase his hours to help pay for school and said he was still short on tuition and money for books. I asked him about financial aid, but he said his dad's income was making it difficult for him to get aid, even though his dad lived out of state and did not support him. I talked to him about transferring to Ohio State. Having once worked as an academic advisor, I knew that four-year institutions had more financial options for students, so that in the long run it might be slightly more expensive, but it would make it possible for him to stay in school. He was disgruntled with my advice and angry at what he perceived to be a hopeless situation. Ryan had been looking forward to college, and it pained me to hear that it too was a struggle for him. I had hoped it would provide the academic challenge he longed for and the financial and emotional support he needed. I took his phone number, thinking that we could reconnect later for a member check, but we have not spoken since.

"We Really Believe They Can Do It": How Freshman Teachers View Urban Students on Their Own Terms

During my interview with the freshman humanities teachers, Mr. Springer and Mrs. Scott, I was caught off guard by their attitude toward the students. Prior to this conversation, most teachers and parents talked about students within the dichotomy of either academically motivated or personally disinterested. After being at OMS for over six months, I realized that there was a difference between the 9th grade humanities classroom and the upper grades. I made the following field notes while observing them in the spring:

> *I am struck by their attitudes toward their students. Something changes between freshman and later grades. Students change or teachers change. Expectations change. But these teachers believe that everyone can succeed.*

Mr. Springer and Mrs. Scott were not plagued by the mindset I heard from others who worked with the upperclassmen and perceived lower expectations for college prep students and higher expectations for others. They worked in racially diverse, mixed ability classrooms. I firmly believe that it was in part their attitude toward students as learners and their willingness to bring each student further down the academic road while setting high expectations that laid a firm foundation for students. The following excerpts from our interview strikingly demonstrate their commitment to seeing their students as agents in their own education:

Sara: Do all students in the class rise to the challenge? Is it more of a slow progression? Coming from all over the district, how do they acclimate to your expectations?

Mrs. Scott: They do at different levels and different speeds. It's difficult . . . it would never be possible to get every 9th grader that walked through the door ready for 10th grade academia in OMS in their freshman year. *I know for certain that we believe strongly that we get every student the same distance forward, they just may not end up at the same spot academically.* And we really strongly believe that our program in 9th grade is stronger than any other program in 9th grade in probably the city, which sounds arrogant, but if we didn't believe that we'd change it. So whether it's accurate or not, we really believe it—*that what we're doing for them is giving them a skeleton for success and they can't all go at the same pace because none of the middle schools are aligned at all.* There are lottery middle schools, arts focused middle schools, private middle schools that they come from, so they're all prepared at different levels. It's impossible to come in and say that we could get them all to the same academic spot. *There is resistance from students who aren't as prepared for 9th grade and so it's inevitable, and we know that. But we know for sure they are further along with us than they would have been without us.*

Mr Springer: They do come from all over. There are some kids from certain middle schools that typically are going to be better prepared than others, *but we still have the same expectations of all the kids.* We expect the kids to do a certain thing or to be able to perform at a certain level and so we hang those high expectations in front of them. *Some we have to help more than others and some we have to push along a little more than others. What I've notice since I've been here, the kids that are more reluctant or it takes a little longer for them to catch on, there's always a point in the year when you definitely can see a change in them* . . . It's usually a particular unit that they like more than others when everything finally comes together for them. Whether the student gets to be more organized—because that's a big problem too—organization skills. Sometimes it's just a certain unit *that captures their attention more than others that makes them realize how all the pieces fit together.*

There are some kids who unfortunately may have to fail the class and they may not get there until their sophomore year. *They may have struggled through their freshman year, but they'll come back and you'll realize what's happened when they learn from their mistakes and they're ready to go the next year.* So it may take a year of struggling for some kids. But I think the expectations are so high. *The theory is if you have high expectations the kids will rise to those expectations, and I think what we've been doing proves that.*

Mrs. Scott: Our kids, *I think they're aware that we really know they can do it. It's not lip service. We really believe they can.*

They also recognized that it was structural disadvantages and students' limited access to skills that affected their potential to succeed at OMS, and not lack of intelligence, interest, motivation, or desire:

> Mrs. Scott: Most of the time, almost all of the time, when a student isn't prepared in their 9th grade year for what we're giving them that first month, it's because *they haven't had access to the skills.* It's not because they can't. *It's our job to give them access to the skills and allow them to go at their own pace with us, but it's not an option for them to not do it.* They may just not do it at the same pace as everyone else, and they understand that we are always going to expect them to rise to those goals that we have for them. *We really believe they can do it.*

Yet they also believed that there were some students that the school was failing by allowing them to struggle when another school might serve them better, and they perceived that they were getting more of these students each year:

> Mrs. Scott: It's clear that we have more students coming unprepared for their 9th grade year. They are not students that can't do the work, but they definitely aren't fully prepared. They are put at a severe disadvantage by their families who may be making a decision in some cases to send them to this school for other than academic reasons. We struggle with that as a staff, because we understand the reasoning behind the parent's decision, but sometimes students are at such a disadvantage that no matter how much remediation we provide for them, it appears by their senior year they're still not able to catch up for some reason.

However, they argued that students who were "capable" and "willing" could still be academically successful at OMS:

> Mrs. Scott: Our goal is to not have remedial courses in this school. We have never and our goal is to never. Because we really want to remain an alternative program for students in public school who are *capable* in 9th grade of doing the work that we're asking *or willing* in 9th grade. *Both of those categories are fair to ask our students. If you're not capable but willing, we think we can get you there.* If you are unwilling and aren't able in the 9th grade . . . *When I say capable I mean come ready, not can't; if you are not ready academically, but you are willing we can get you there.*

In their talk of students, they recognized the structural inequalities that persist in the district that may put students at a disadvantage, but they unfixed students from the urban discourses that situated them as culturally disadvantaged, purposefully disinterested, or intrinsically unmotivated. Their explanations for under-achievement shifted from the students to the educational system, and as educators, they assume the responsibility of bringing students farther along their academic path by setting high expectations and providing the skills needed to succeed. Their statements were peppered with indications that they accepted students on their own terms—moving them forward while knowing that they will not all reach the same place, pushing some a little more than others, allowing them to go at their own pace but expecting them to do the work, and watching the pieces fit together.

Erica, a freshman that I interviewed, recognized the importance of having these teachers and the impact they could have on students and their futures:

> But at OMS, the teachers keep trying to help you, keep trying to enforce that education is important, and that's not something that you try to give up on. I think it's all about the decision to try and accept the fact that someone's helping you . . . If you accept the help that you're getting I think that will bring [you] up to the point where [you'll] recognize education is important.

While some of these students would move into basic college prep courses and experience lowered expectations, I believe that the foundation they received in the 9th grade, the high expectations and the belief that they could do it, carried them through their four years and encouraged them to hold onto college aspirations. I end here with a quote from Tanesha, a student in Mr. Fisher's split course, who also worked full time and supported her family financially. Tanesha saw herself as "smart" and recognizes the possibilities of OMS, regardless of how others saw her, the classes in which she is enrolled, or the circumstances of her life outside of school:

Tanesha: He's a really good teacher even though he jokes a lot. Because the jokes are educational. And that's another way *you find out how smart you are*, because you're laughing at an educational joke. Everybody's like "oh yeah, I get it."

Sara: You feel like you realized how smart you were when you came here?

Tanesha: Yeah, I realized. I was getting As and Bs since kindergarten. I think through middle school I didn't realize how much I really learned, but I did learn a lot. So here, and being in humanities, *you realize how much you learn* from the books and everything. Like I'm watching TV and they say something about a book we read at

> school . . . because we read *The Invisible Man*. And they read a quote out of that book that I did my report on. And I'm sitting there like "OMS does a lot!" And my mom's like "What?" "Nothing mom, you wouldn't understand, because it's about school." "You're probably gonna be a little nerd," she says. I tell my mom, "Nerds make all the money," because my mom calls me a nerd.

Conclusion

OMS is in many ways an example of urban public schooling at its best, and I attribute much of their success to the strength of their humanities program, the culture of high expectations perpetuated by the school, and their commitment to meaningful teaching and learning focused on college preparation and attainment. These factors allowed the school to subvert the constraining effects of NCLB and circumvent the impact of high stakes testing by offering academic achievement on their own terms and not solely on the state's terms. Their students fared better, went farther, and the experiences they shared were a testament to the possibilities of public education.

Through these practices, OMS established itself as an academic high school, and surprisingly it was situated as an "alternative" to traditional public education, though academics should be the norm of every school. The idea of "academics as the alternative" calls into question the expectations we have for secondary education and for students. What allows the academic climate of a school to be undermined? How might secondary education reclaim academics in its mission?

This book articulates the meaning of race in public education today and looks at how race in many ways disrupted the excellent intentions of OMS. In spite of the school's excellent intentions, practices of enrollment were embedded within a grid of racialized discourses about urban students that justified the overrepresentation of students of color in college preparation courses and placed responsibility for course selection largely on the students. Parents and school staff situated this pattern as an effect of individual choice and identified other colorblind reasons for this racial stratification. Faculty and staff performed practices that discouraged students from taking academic risks and enrolling in AP or International Baccalaureate (IB) courses, and these practices had effects along lines of race and class.

Yet, race was manipulated and negotiated by schooling actors in complicated and competing ways. Parents and students worked discourses of urban identity to their advantage. The school utilized its urban cachet to receive recognition and awards that often benefited the students, the school, and the district. Black parents used this urban cachet to gain acceptance at competitive colleges, while white parents took a sense of pride in bending their white privilege by sending their student to a predominantly Black high school. The discourses of urban identity remained unchallenged though by these manipulations, which tended to maintain and stabilize urban students within the discourses of cultural disadvantage, risk, and poverty.

By looking closer at the material experiences of "urban" students at OMS, we begin to see through their elusive and slippery negotiations that they are quite capable of becoming educational subjects on their own terms. They show us that part of being an urban student at a high-achieving school is working to negotiate the lived experiences of structural disadvantage within and against the discursive, historical, and social constraints of education. Their ambivalence in the on-going process of becoming educational subjects is marked by the ways in which they exceed taken-for-granted constructions of urban identity. The analysis of these portraits shifted our gaze to *the absent traces* of raced and classed structural inequalities that are ignored when talking about urban students. The negotiations of Natasha, Ryan, Esther, and other students opened up the restricted binary formulation of "those students" versus "successful students." Their subjectivity offers a transgression of the imposed boundaries and categorizations to demonstrate how living is both historically and socially contingent, but also an unbounded process through which students invest in, divest, and disrupt identity. They allow us to glimpse how they negotiated the lived experiences and discursive constraints of success and achievement as *educational agents and subjects on their own terms.*

References

Fine, M. (1995). The politics of who's at risk. In B. Blue Swadener and S. Lubeck (Eds.), *Children and Families at Promise: Deconstructing the Discourse of Risk* (pp. 76–94). Albany, NY: State University of New York Press.

Yon, D. (2000). *Elusive Culture: Schooling, Race, and Identity in Global Times*. Albany, NY: State University of New York Press.

CONCLUSION

At the beginning of this study I stated that I had two goals in mind: 1) to examine how critical schooling actors at OMS practiced complex systems of educational policies to better understand the effects of policy on everyday teaching and learning; and 2) to explore the ways race continues to work in US public schools and attempt through this text to unfix students of color from the overburdened discourses of urban identity to see them as educational agents *on their own terms*.

This conclusion will substantively address the contributions a study like this might make to the field of ethnographic policy analysis, urban educational research, and qualitative research by reviewing the key conceptual findings and the methodological and theoretical implications of this study. In conclusion, I want to address the failures of the No Child Left Behind (NCLB) Act as an equity reform, the effects of our educational debt on student achievement, and possibilities for equity and excellence when we view students as educational agents on their own terms.

Substantive Implications

Policy as Practice

This case study bridged a theorized analysis of race with an explicitly ethnographic study of policy as practice. As such, it interrogated the sociocultural manifestations of NCLB as negotiated by critical school actors and highlighted how they subverted the constraining effects of NCLB in ways that supported the academic success and achievement of their students. This research also exposed the punishing policy practices of the district that undermined the school's academic climate of high expectations. Practices of credit recovery and increased enrollment became strategies employed by the district as they attempted to comply with the bottom line of standards and accountability—numbers, test scores, and graduation rates—the terms of the state. The *policy as practice* framework served as a useful tool to expose the complicated workings and negotiations of policy on the ground. It provided a careful analysis of how policy is practiced at the local level by teachers and administrators, the daily negotiations they undertake to protect academic excellence and promote equity, and the power relations that are manifested within accountability that have a punishing effect on schools.

Urban Cachet

In Chapter 5 I defined the concept of urban cachet that refers to the sense of identity, specialness, and prestige garnered by identifying as an "urban" student or school, and I described how this cachet was put into practice by Ohio Magnet School, parents, and students. I identified three uses of urban cachet that required a construction of urban students as objects to be contained, displayed, or transformed by education: 1) the commodification of this cachet to gain recognition, grants, and awards which supported student success and shored up depleted school resources; 2) African American parents' purposeful use of this cachet to improve their students' chances for admission to prestigious universities; and 3) the convergence of urban cachet with white privilege and liberal desire that constructed their students' enrollment in OMS as a political investment in diversity. While these three manipulations of urban cachet had productively positive effects for students—increasing school resources, opportunities, and diversity—they fixed, displayed, and capitalized on the discourse of the urban student as other.

Each form of cachet utilizes a construction of urban educational identity overburdened by discourses of disadvantage and risk. These negotiations of urban cachet demonstrated how urban students and schools are discursively constructed through cultural assumptions that attribute student failure to students themselves. These power/knowledge relations are productive of multiple effects that require and desire this particular brand of urban educational other to function, and each retraces the limits of the identity in its reproduction. Without its urban education other, the achievement at OMS would not be so surprising or worthy of recognition. It is the expectations of low achievement from students of color, the discursive relations of whiteness/achievement and Blackness/failure, which give OMS its referential power. As demonstrated by participants' inability to address the role that race and identity played or to recognize how these practices were sustained by real and imagined lived experiences of students of color, urban cachet was a de-raced practice particularly for the school and white families. The value of cachet as a commodity and the use of it to do good things for students elided the complexities of race, socioeconomics, and educational disadvantage that sustained it.

On Their Own Terms

By seeing students at OMS as urban educational subjects *on their own terms* I strived to demonstrate how students were agents in the making, remaking, and resisting of identity and education. I resisted the desire of ethnography to believe it can know subjects completely or portray them with uninterrupted accuracy. Rather I recognized that identity was elusive, active, and on the move, and experienced it as such as I got to know students. These experiences gave way to a desire to work against the legacy of social science research that continuously reproduced urban students within these stagnant discourses of risk, deprivation, and disadvantage. The hard work came in attempting to represent the unhinging of dominant and local discourses in writing and allow the portrayals of these students to stay open and yet also allow in the material effects of race and socioeconomic inequality that impacted their lives. The portraits of Natasha, Esther, Ryan, and Tanesha, and the insights gathered from across the study, demonstrated how students' negotiations slide in and out of traditional discourses of urban identity. These slippages gave way to an understanding of urban subjectivity that demonstrated how students inhabit, reappropriate, and puncture the containment of identity to negotiate success and achievement on their own terms.

This analysis engaged with the materiality of students' lives as urban subjects who negotiate academics with the real needs to support themselves and their families financially. They worked to pay for housing, phone bills, and food while saving for college and attempting to stay on top of their academic workloads. These raced and classed structural inequalities, not inherent cultural traits or intrinsic abilities, directly impacted their course choices, homework completion, and class participation. By unhinging discourses of cultural disadvantage from urban student identity and reconceptualizing students on their own terms, I lastly wanted to *shift educational responsibility back to schools, districts, and the state.*

Theoretical and Methodological Implications

The Re-Invention of Urban Education

The historical construction of urban identity inside and outside of social science research is more than just troubling: it represents the constant (re)presenting and fixing of real people within racialized discourses that locate disadvantage, risk, and poverty as functions of an individual's race and culture. I attempted to conduct a genealogy of urban identity and the complicit role that even well-meaning social science research played in the "containment and display" of urban communities and students to not only recognize but hold my feet to the fire as I wrote. Through a historical analysis, I attempted to locate a different historical "starting" point within the history of successful African American education and a long legacy of education for freedom. Not that I can escape the inherent damage of research, but I found it imperative to attempt to find a different location from which to begin and hold myself accountable. To start from the very place that contains African American students and students of color and fixes, and solidifies what we think we know about their educational engagement, does nothing but further contribute to their marginalization.

Tightening and Loosening Theory

At the same time, I wanted to undermine any expectations that I could liberate either myself or this study from the trappings of racialization. I fully acknowledge that I cannot escape the ways in which race works in research, regardless of my attempts to disrupt the power/knowledge relations of race in my project. That being said, I think there is something powerfully important about "doing it and troubling it simultaneously" (Lather, 2007), and about moving out of the paralysis that ensues when trying to do socially just research about and with others.

I relied on a diverse set of theoretical and methodological frameworks to make specific shifts and interventions into policy work and gestured toward a feminist post-critical methodology to do policy work differently. I engaged the theoretical tensions and methodological frictions at play to move me through ethical suspensions and emotionally troubling spaces. Specifically, I put critical race theory (CRT) in education in direct conversations with poststructural/post-critical theories to *tighten and loosen* frameworks. This tightening and loosening was not for novelty's sake; it was about using theory to promote and trouble ethical engagement, to keep the work moving while troubling it every step of the way. CRT held me accountable to naming race and privilege; it tightened poststructural theory to make use of the materiality of urban students' experiences and bring structural inequality to bear on the analysis. As such, race mattered and was a privileged site of working poststructural theory. Simultaneously, poststructural theory performed a loosening of CRT, reading structural inequalities along the lines of power/knowledge that are held within them, identifying both the limits and the productive possibilities, and using the loosened reading to unhinge and unfix urban student identity to think differently about students as educational agents on their own terms. I believe it was the engagement with methodologically diverse approaches, whose friction engaged serious critique, that made possible the recognition of practices like urban cachet, as it was able to tease out the role that identity played and yet move beyond static criticism to see the productive effects of the practices that were simultaneously useful and troubling.

Again, the implications of tightening and loosening theory were about making ethical moves that use the power of theory while placing these theories in direct conversation with their overriding critiques continuously to disrupt their own fixed and troubling tendencies. Each framework has use, and each framework requires continuous critique to be useful. This useful troubling then is in the name of a more accountable social science.

Deconstructive/Disruptive Practices of Research

I used Derridean deconstruction as an analytic practice to keep the study open to the anomalies, complications, and "outliers" typically left behind, scrapped, or trimmed off for another day. I utilized deconstruction to privilege the messiness of everyday teaching and learning and tap into it as the very energy and product of research. This style of analysis led me toward a series of substantive findings that exposed both the productive effects and the limits of policy as/in practice and the workings of race in schools.

Feminist Post-Critical Policy Analysis

I have attempted to use feminist post-critical policy analysis as a tool to be of both trouble and use. Shifting its gaze from the macro to the micro, this study engaged a *policy as practice* framework while bringing feminist critique to bear. It took seriously Marshall's (1997) call to focus research on the local level and extended this idea by privileging its usefulness on the ground. The focus on everyday practice shifted from the goals of traditional macro-level policymakers to assess implementation to instead privilege the lived experiences of local policy-actors. I do not buy into the romance of data-driven policy formation; neither do I have any expectations to be useful at the macro level of policymaking and politics. My intention was to engage more complex questions about how policy is negotiated and put to work in the local arena, with the hopes that it would be useful for schools and communities. Equally, this study problematized a feminist critical tradition of heavy-handed critique and sought a more nuanced relationship with its data that is invested in both the productive effects *and* limits of policy as practice. I have also not shied away from making recommendations, but I trouble the translation, applicability, and "implementation" of recommendations. I am more interested as a feminist post-critical policy researcher in the ways in which recommendations are engaged as power and knowledge, used, negotiated, and critiqued in the everyday practices of teaching and learning.

The Failures of NCLB as Equity Reform: How Race Works in Schools

In conclusion, I lastly argue that the federal policy of NCLB fails as an equity reform. In spite of the rhetoric of policy and the intentions of some policymakers to close the achievement gap, NCLB functions as an accountability and standards reform that assumes equity to be a byproduct of success that is measured by test scores. It fails to acknowledge the structural inequalities that critical actors face every day that impact teaching and learning, and it shifts responsibility away from the state and back onto students, parents, teachers, and cultures.

As we see at OMS, though the school was effective in closing the achievement gap, it continued to expose the limits of excellence and the inability of NCLB to promote educational equity and access to opportunity for students of color and poor students. Standards and accountability, the terms of the state, effectively delimited the very excellence of OMS' curriculum and climate through practices of credit recovery and graduation test preparation. Race policed the boundaries of excellence through racialized enrollments that marginalized students of color from AP and IB courses, and elided the structural inequalities that affected students through *color blind discourses* and *discourses of individual choice.* In spite of the school's ability to meet the terms of the state by closing the achievement gap and the empowerment it did offer students, equity itself was an elusive goal, something glimpsed but not fully realized.

As Ladson-Billings (2006) argues, the US preoccupation with the achievement gap and the narrowing of the gap through educational reforms locates the problem within individual students, teachers, schools, families, and communities, and offers merely short-term solutions to long-term inequality. Rather than an achievement gap, she argues that the US has accumulated an *educational debt* that has been shouldered largely by students of color and their communities who have been deprived of educational and other resources leading to persistent and pervasive educational inequality. In one way, OMS demonstrated the continued impact of this debt in spite of its best intentions to do otherwise. Despite the fact that equity and educational achievement were at the core of this school's mission, race worked indelibly within and against practices of successes. Statistically, the gap was closed and arguably repaid some of this debt by increasing aspirations, graduation, and college entrance, but in practice much of this debt remained in the discursive constructions of urban identity and the overrepresentation of students of color in college prep courses.

So how might OMS point toward a more complicated understanding of tensions between equity and excellence? What might we learn about how better to serve students from their wrestlings with the materiality of these tensions? What concrete practices can be put in place? How might we divest from privilege? And how can we begin to see students on their own terms? In spite of our desires to believe otherwise in the US, race continues to matter in schools. It matters in the creation and implementation of educational policy. It matters in practice and the everyday lives of teachers and students. Despite its rhetorical focus on the disadvantaged and minority students, NCLB fails as an equity reform, because it functions as a colorblind reform that ignores structural inequalities along lines of race and class while simultaneously asserting a reform colored by whiteness, choice, and a belief in merit unburdened by discrimination or systemic disadvantage. Race is both meaningless and meaningful. Under NCLB, minority students *can fail on their own terms, but they cannot achieve on their own terms.*

For NCLB to succeed as an equity reform, it must attend to the structural inequalities that exist for students and center equity within its mandates, measures, and enforcement. At the same time, we need to begin to see students on their own terms, as educational agents that negotiate inequality, opportunity, and achievement. By starting from a different position that privileges a critical engagement with the effects of race historically and presently on students and schools, I hope this bearing witness to knowledge that is difficult and unsettling will bring us closer to meeting our expectations for a more just and democratic education.

References

Ladson-Billings, G. (2006). From the achievement gap to the education debt: Understanding achievement in U.S. schools. *Educational Researcher, 35*(7), 3–12.

Lather, P. (2007). *Getting Lost: Feminist Efforts toward a Doubled Science.* Albany, NY: State University of New York Press.

Marshall, C. (Ed.). (1997). *Feminist Critical Policy Analysis I: A Perspective from Primary and Secondary Schooling* (Vol. 1). London: The Falmer Press.

No Child Left Behind Act, 20 U.S.C. § 6301, (2001).

APPENDIX I

Getting in Trouble

When I walked through the doors of Ohio Magnet School (OMS) in the fall of 2008, I immediately felt like I was back in high school. I had never been a troublemaker, but as an anxious rule-follower, my fear of getting in trouble was constant. The same anxiety crept back into my body once I crossed the threshold of OMS. It didn't matter that I was a 34-year-old contributing member of society with two children, a mortgage, and other adult responsibilities. I looked for a trashcan to spit out my gum, and, worried that I would be questioned for roaming the halls, I headed straight to the office to sign in and get a visitor's badge.

I recognized early on that my *fear* of messing up during fieldwork was going to be more of a barrier than any mistake I might make. Messing up, or getting in trouble, was also not something I could completely control. I decided then that I was already 'in trouble' as a researcher, and this idea became a source of methodological energy as opposed to paralyzing anxiety.

The idea of 'trouble' works well in school settings—detention, suspension, or calls to the Principal's office. Getting into trouble became a way to break the tension of anxieties. If there is no way to get it all right, then it is important to find satisfaction in what comes from the field. Rather than having expectations for complete rapport and total comfort while observing and interviewing, it was methodologically useful to think about the potential for being 'in trouble' with participants: in a state of tension and disagreement regarding my coming to know them fully through ethnography. Accepting that misrecognition and misunderstanding were part of working with and learning about the lives of real people, I found these places of unknowing to be useful and interesting. It challenged me to ask more questions of my participants and myself.

I also positioned trouble as unavoidable, that part of the work of research is 'getting into trouble,' and I hoped to find joy rather than sadness in this kind of failing. Getting into trouble was permission to take risks and look for the interruptions at work in the empirical materials, not just look for consistency, cohesion, or pretty stories. When I began to ask questions about the overrepresentation of Black students in basic courses, I was immediately disciplined by some participants for raising the issue. However, recognizing that this reaction was part of doing research, it was easier to accept these kinds of confrontations and move through them.

For as much as I metaphorically used this idea of trouble to keep me moving, I also relied on traditional modes of qualitative inquiry to conduct the study and evaluate my own practice. I provide a discussion of my methodological approach to ethnographic research and grounded theory, followed by a nuts-and-bolts description of the study.

A Note on Ethnographic Methods

Educational ethnographies are characterized as "research on and in educational institutions based on participant observation and/or permanent recordings of everyday life" (Delamont and Atkinson, 1995, p. 15, cited in Gordon, Holland, & Lahelma, 2001). Participant observation is a core activity of ethnography and involves prolonged engagement with the field site and immersion of the researcher into the social world of one's subjects. Field notes are intended to serve as a written production of experience that is contemporaneous, selective, descriptive, and cumulative (Emerson, Fretz, & Shaw, 2001). I was more observer than participant in most instances, and while I was involved with this school for a considerable amount of time, my prolonged engagement did not measure up to the yardstick of more archetypal anthropological studies. However, I also resist being completely "disciplined" by the discipline of traditional ethnography (Gonzalez, 2004), and prefer an "ethnography of ruins" (Lather, 2001). I am suspicious of standards that use reified notions of culture, subject/object, researcher, field, or representation to authoritatively define how knowledge ought to be produced through ethnography, when each and every field site has its own materiality and relationality (Childers, 2013). That does not mean anything goes. It means that the methodological approach of this study was made with great care and consideration for the specificities of the field sites and participants.

I consider the field to be not only the material school location experienced by participants and myself but also a "product" of my interaction and writing that is constructed in and through the inscription and transcription process. It is multi-sited and includes "discursive textual, visual, and archival historical materials and documents, as well as ethnographic (interview and observational) transcripts and field notes to more fully take into account the complexities of postmodern life" (Clarke, 2005, p.xxxiii). The school itself served as the primary location, but the field expanded beyond the walls of the school into offices, libraries, parking lots, and coffee shops, and also accounted for documents and materials that expanded the situation of inquiry.

I always carried a steno notebook with me and openly recorded field notes during my observations and interviews. By the end of the year, I had filled four of these notebooks, which were elaborated on and typed up daily, equaling over 100 pages when typed. There were occasions when conversations with teachers or students turned into informal interviews. Rather than interrupt the conversation by digging around in my bag for my journal or asking if I could turn on my digital recorder, these were later recorded by hand in my journal, usually in a bathroom stall, the stairwell, or my car, once the conversations were over.

My field journal was both observational and reflexive. The reflexive journal component of ethnography, while considered important, is often situated as outside the genre of ethnography or relegated to the appendices of studies. Van Maanen (1988) warns of the dangers of "vanity ethnography" and confessional tales that stall the original intent of research, that of describing and interpreting the happenings of others (p. 93). However, writers like Laurel Richardson (1997), Ruth Behar (1993), and Carolyn Ellis (2004), write the researcher and the process of representation back into ethnographic projects. While my presence may not be felt much in the book, I want to be clear that my experiences and ethical wrestlings served as fertile fodder for the methodological and theoretical decisions I made; therefore, they were not relegated to a disenfranchised location in my hard drive, but were intermingled with field notes and vignettes.

A More Situated Inquiry

Glaser and Strauss (2006/1967) defined grounded theory as a general method of comparative analysis for "the discovery of theory from data." Clarke (2005) revised grounded theory, "pushing and pulling" it around the postmodern turn into a method she refers to as situational analysis. She critiqued it for a lack of reflexivity, an oversimplification of the data that strains toward coherence, a singular rather than multiple process, a view of variation as "negative case," and its reliance on positivist objectivity (pp. 11–18). Clarke proposed, "to supplement basic grounded theory with a situation-centered approach that in addition to studying action also explicitly includes the analysis of the full situation, including discourses—narrative, visual, and historical" (p. xxxii).

Situated analysis recuperated grounded theories' positivist leanings by: 1) explicitly acknowledging the embodiment and situatedness of all knowledge producers and assuming the multiplicity of knowledges; 2) grounding the phenomenon of study in the broader situation—Clarke defines the situation as both ecological and relational; it includes all the major human, non-human, discursive, and other elements of relation and the on-going negotiations and positions taken and not taken in the situation of inquiry (pp. xxii, 21–23); 3) shifting from assumptions of normativity and homogeneity to complexities, differences, and heterogeneities; 4) focusing on the process of theorizing and the development of sensitizing concepts as opposed to the pursuit of a formal theory; and 5) turning to discourses to expand the sites of inquiry (p. 19).

Clarke proposed a systematic process that used situational mapping to document the connections between situational elements as the main strategy of analysis. I did not formally utilize her mapping method. While early on I sketched out situational, social world, and positional maps to move discursive, historical, social, and material contexts from background to foreground, I did not use them strictly as my main analytic strategy, and I do not supply those maps here. I was inspired by Clarke's theorizing of the research process as one of embodiment, relationality, multiple knowledges, complexities, differences, heterogeneity, and variations. It served as a resource that envisioned how to bring traditional data sources around the postmodern turn. As detailed in the first two chapters of this book, I used particular theoretical lenses and philosophical approaches to analyze and make sense of the complexities at work in the lives of students at OMS.

Access

Gaining full access to OMS took longer than anticipated due to the hiring of a new Principal. During the summer months, while I waited for her approval, I conducted background research and gathered policy documents for preliminary analysis. Once approved, the school was very willing to allow me into the building, and once the school police officer was familiar with my face, I was able to move about freely. Both the Principal, Dr. Davis, and my teacher liaison, Mr. Fisher, held doctorates and were therefore research friendly. They also felt that the research could be positive for the school. Mr. Fisher expressed that he wanted "to have time to reflect, and being prompted to discuss the school and/or my practice forced me to set time aside to self examine." There was an admitted interest in showcasing the good work of the school and the teachers, particularly because of the negative attention teachers and teaching received in the current climate of accountability. They were also very interested in how the findings could support their work and how they might serve as a model for other schools.

Slicing up the Case Study

At first, I decided to cast a wide net in regards to data collection, and I left myself open to experiences and interactions. For example, the lunchroom might seem like an unnecessary location for observations about classroom practice, but it allowed me to see student relationships outside the classroom and gave me an opportunity to chat with students about school culture and their lives without the pressures of a formal interview. In an attempt to "make the familiar strange" (Erickson, 1986), I focused on rich, thick descriptions of the school, the participants, and the myriad interactions, but as the study went on I narrowed my focus.

I used various sampling strategies and methods of data collection to create "slices of data" (Glaser & Strauss, 2006/1967) and multiple views of the policy appropriation process. I sliced out of the case multiple data sources creating a corpus that consisted of field notes, interview and focus group transcripts, email correspondences, and an archive of educational policy documents, print articles, high school yearbooks, and school and PTA websites. I broke the case study down into smaller samples of events or *situations* that I wanted to observe, critical actors that I wanted to interview, and policies and documents that I wanted to review.

I carried out nine consecutive months of fieldwork, visiting the school three or four days a week and spending anywhere from three to six hours observing and interviewing. After an initial immersion into the culture of the school through 12 weeks of intense observation across all grades and programs, I focused my participant observation on a cross section of courses in the humanities program and continued observations through the end of the school year, June 2009. The humanities program served as a purposeful sample from which to start, because all students were required to take one social studies course each year. Courses were offered at the basic college preparation, Advanced Placement (AP), and International Baccalaureate (IB) levels, giving me access to students across the three curriculums and four grades. I was invited to school events such as the winter formal assembly, plays, senior breakfast, and other activities as they occurred.

The school supported my recruitment efforts. Teachers were made aware of my study and became accustomed to my presence quickly. Only one teacher declined classroom observations, though she did participate in an interview. I interviewed and/or observed nine teachers. Five of the nine teachers taught social studies at different levels and in different curriculum tracks. I broadened this sample by observing and/or interviewing a Spanish teacher, the librarian, a special education teacher, and the art teacher. I observed an AP chemistry class taught by the IB theory of knowledge teacher already in my sample. I also intentionally sought out the only two African American teachers at the school.

Student participants were gathered via snowball sampling, theoretical sampling, and random sampling. I provided incentives for participation by way of food, typically pizza or McDonalds, and a $5 gift card to a local bookstore. Students volunteered, and I scheduled individual interviews and focus groups during their lunch periods or after school. I sent out consent forms and received 18 back, and 13 students were interviewed. Within a few weeks of conducting interviews, I determined that I needed to actively recruit more students of color, particularly Black males, as well as students taking AP and IB courses, to fill general gaps in the demographic make up of the sample as well as to explore some hunches. Mr. Fisher helped me to identify students in his first period study hall that met these criteria, and four more students agreed to be interviewed during this time. Though I interviewed two male students, one African American and one white, males represent a gap in my interview sample.

I interviewed 11 parents individually or via focus groups, 8 white females, 1 African American female, and 2 African American males. They were parents of both male and female students in different grade levels and programs. Because I could not identify parents who met particular criteria, I utilized a variety of strategies to contact them about the study to generate a purposeful sample. I attended and spoke at a PTA meeting and collected the contact information of parents who were interested in participating. The PTA included information about my study in their newsletter that goes out to all dues-paying members and some parents contacted me after reading this. The parent consultant also published on three occasions a solicitation for my study along with the schedule of upcoming focus groups in the weekly email newsletter sent to all parents at the school.

I scheduled three focus groups that coincided with evening PTA meetings that were held at various locations in the city. Seven parents were interviewed in focus groups. Four also took me up on my offer to interview them individually at a time and location convenient to them. The entire parent sample was comprised of parents who were actively involved in the PTA, with the exception of one parent who was a dues-paying member but did not attend meetings. Solicitations in the weekly newsletter failed to generate the participation of parents not in the PTA. I also used the student consent form as an opportunity to solicit participation from this demographic. Four parents indicated their interest, but they did not respond to requests to set up interviews.

I endeavored to interview all administrators and non-teaching academic staff. My sample includes the Principal, one of the two Assistant Principals, both guidance counselors, the school police officer, and one parent consultant. I had informal contact with several special education aids and the school security officer during the year. Due to time constraints and availability, I did not interview the internship coordinator or any external program representatives that had limited contact with the school. I also excluded non-academic staff such as custodians, cafeteria workers, and office staff.

In spite of my best efforts, there were "the ones that got away," participants whose interviews were difficult for me to capture during the course of the study. Boys served a sizable gap, and AP and IB students proved disinterested in participating. There were also several individual students I wished to interview. For example, I could not secure interviews with Esther and Cody, two students who were prevalent in my field notes. On the day I had finally gotten Esther on the calendar, I arrived to school to find out she had been suspended. I experienced this as both a loss and lost: a loss of important voices and stories, and lost opportunities to further explore, expand, and add nuance to this project. However, their presence was evident throughout my observational notes.

The document archive comprised 50 policy and non-policy documents. In the early stages of my project, I did a great deal of research on federal, state, and district policies related to OMS. These documents were key in compiling data tables and locating policies that framed practice. I also reviewed yearbooks and collected newspaper and magazine articles, editorials, and related media that discussed the school, its awards, or its impact on the community and provided sources of social, historical, and discursive context. School and PTA websites were also used as documents to map activities and practices. Throughout the data collection, I built an archive of curriculum materials, district pacing guides, and scheduling guides that were included in the analysis.

This first portion of my fieldwork ended in June 2009 at the conclusion of the school year. Each participant was given the option of reviewing and requesting changes to their transcript, but none were made. In December 2009 I was invited back to OMS by the PTA to answer questions about how they might respond to some changes being initiated by the district that they feared would negatively impact their program. Their invitation led to three member checks that occurred between December and March, first with a small group of PTA parents, followed by a meeting with the school advisory board comprised of administrators, parents, and teachers, and then lastly they permitted me to meet with the entire school staff of 40. I shared the results of my study and asked for feedback, as well as answered their questions about how they might use the data to support their program.

References

Behar, R. (1993). *Translated Woman: Crossing the Border with Esperanza's Story*. Boston, MA: Beacon Press.

Childers, S. M. (2013). The materiality of fieldwork: Ontology of feminist becoming. *International Journal of Qualitative Studies in Education, 26*(5), pp. 507–622.

Clarke, A. E. (2005). *Situational Analysis: Grounded Theory after the Postmodern Turn*. Thousand Oaks, CA: Sage Publications.

Delamont, S., & Atkinson, P. (1995). *Fighting Familiarity: Essays on Education and Ethnography*. Cresskill, NJ: Hampton Press.

Ellis, C. (2004). *The Ethnographic I: A Methodological Novel about Autoethnography*. Walnut Creek, CA: AltaMira Press.

Emerson, R. M., Fretz, R. I., & Shaw, L. L. (2001). Participant observation and fieldnotes. In P. Atkinson, A. Coffey, S. Delamont, J. Lofland, and L. Lofland (Eds.), *Handbook of Ethnography* (pp. 352–368). London: Sage Publications.

Erickson, F. (1986). Qualitative methods in research on teaching. In W. C. Wittrock (Ed.), *Handbook of Research on Teaching* (3rd ed., pp. 119–161). New York: Macmillan.

Glaser, B. G., & Strauss, A. L. (2006/1967). *The Discovery of Grounded Theory: Strategies for Qualitative Research*. New Brunswick, NJ: Aldine Transaction. (Original work published 1967.)

Gonzalez, N. (2004). Disciplining the discipline: Anthropology and the pursuit of quality education. *Educational Researcher, 33*(5), 17–25.

Gordon, T., Holland, J., & Lahelma, E. (2001). Ethnographic research in education settings. In P. Atkindons, A. Coffey, S. Delamont, J. Lofland, and L. Lofland (Eds.), *Handbook of Ethnography* (pp. 188–199). London: Sage Publications.

Lather, P. (2001). Ethnography: Of ruins, aporias, and angels. In P. Atkinson, A. Coffey, S. Delamont, J. Lofland, and L. Lofland (Eds.), *Handbook of Ethnography* (pp. 477–492). London: Sage Publications.

Richardson, L. (1997). *Fields of Play: Constructing an Academic Life.* New Brunswick, NJ: Rutgers University Press.

Van Maanen, J. (1988). *Tales of the Field.* Chicago, IL: University of Chicago Press.

APPENDIX II

Recommendations

During the member check I conducted with teachers and staff, I was directly asked for "concrete recommendations" that arose from the data. Out of the desire to be useful, to find use in the data, and reciprocate my appreciation for being allowed to conduct my study at OMS, I sketch possible recommendations here. Teachers and staff were most acutely concerned about the stratification of enrollment at OMS once the data were presented. I believe that teachers and staff make difficult decisions every day about their students, and they do so with life and noise swirling around them. I hope that the study gave them time and opportunity to take a step back momentarily and revisit school issues under quieter and calmer circumstances. I also hope that these ideas might be extrapolated by other schools as potential resolutions to similar issues.

The main recommendation is to define excellence as only possible with equity. That means an excellent school must also achieve racial, economic, and gender parity across its curriculums. If excellence means equity, then both must be explicit in mission and action when it comes to policy and school practice. Therefore, excellence will not just be about test scores or graduation rates, it will also be about access and opportunity. The recommendations below are tangible and explained within the context of OMS; others are about shifting beliefs and thought processes about urban students.

Recommendation 1: Alignment of all middle school curriculums with the College Preparatory Curriculum

Curricular alignment is a district and state responsibility that local schools have little to no control over. I recommend that OMS faculty, staff, and parents advocate for all middle schools to be aligned with OMS, and not just the middle schools that are intended to feed it. Columbus City Schools needs to understand how the under-preparation at the middle school level sets up students for potential failure, not only at OMS but at other area high schools and later in life, as well as the impact of this on graduation rates and standardized test scores.

Recommendation 2: Increase awareness and understanding of prerequisites for AP and IB programs at middle school level and upon entering freshman year

Students and parents made clear that they did not have a firm understanding of the prerequisites for the AP and IB programs. Even those families that felt they were "tracked" into OMS admitted that the path was unclear to them. It is important to not only publicize OMS at the middle school level but also to provide clear information regarding courses that need to be taken before enrollment. This information should be provided to parents and students upon entering middle school, revisited and redistributed each year, and highlighted again when lottery information is provided. The focus here should be on "nuts and bolts" requirements.

Recommendation 3: Clear Articulation Maps for students coming from different academic backgrounds and course planning guides

OMS recognized that students came to the school with different academic backgrounds. This information was taken into consideration internally by faculty and staff when making scheduling decisions for students. Again, many parents and students found the scheduling process to lack transparency and the current scheduling materials that the school provided to be confusing. Clear articulation maps that were externally available to parents and students would be invaluable here. These maps could take two forms: 1) clear and individualized maps that lay out the course paths for each program option at OMS—AP, IB, Seniors to Sophomores, Fort Hayes, Career Center, etc. with prerequisites; and 2) clear and individualized maps for middle schools that clarify the prerequisite courses needed at the middle school level and then how to accelerate or what courses would still be needed once at OMS. These maps would demonstrate course plans for students coming from a more traditional school, a private school, or one of the better-aligned middle schools in the district. They would give students and parents the information they need to make informed decisions and address any scheduling errors. These maps would also serve as advocacy tools for parents that were less likely to engage and for students who were self-reliant in the educational process.

Recommendation 4: AP and IB recruitment

Advertise Widely

The school attempted to advertise AP and IB courses and make students aware of the application process. Students felt that they did not clearly understand the benefits of the program. An in-school assembly would be more time efficient and enable students to get all their questions answered. Continue and increase active recruitment of students of color.

Emphasize Benefit over Rigor

Students and parents felt that the rigor of the courses was emphasized in such a way that it discouraged students from applying. Allow the already understood rigor of the school and the climate of high expectations to continue to be implicit in all courses. Spend time with students emphasizing the benefits of AP and IB in terms of college preparation, college credits, and college costs. Some students also felt counseled away, counseled out, or rejected from the programs. Maintain the level of expectations set for students entering their freshmen year. OMS was already an academic risk for many of them. Encourage them to continue to take those risks.

Eliminate Exclusionary Language in Applications

Students found the language on applications to be exclusionary and discouraging, particularly for students that held jobs or had additional family responsibilities. These students, due to financial considerations, are quite possibly the ones that need access to these opportunities the most. Change or remove language on the applications that suggests that employment or lack of parental engagement guarantees difficulty in succeeding in these courses.

Elevate College Preparation Out of the Hierarchy

Parents and students perceived that the course offerings existed in a hierarchy with IB at the top, college prep at the bottom, and AP in between. Eliminate language and expectations that maintain this hierarchy. Re-establish the college preparation courses as high achieving in the eyes of students and parents while making them aware that the AP and IB courses have additional tests with potential benefits.

Open, Unrestricted Enrollment

Another potential strategy to increase AP and IB enrollment is through open and unrestricted enrollment. Once prerequisites have been verified, allow for open and unrestricted enrollment for all students. Eliminate essay questions to gauge writing skills and other "gatekeeping" strategies that discourage students from taking advantage of AP and IB programming.

Recommendation 5: See students on their own terms

Carry High Expectations into all Classrooms

Students perceived that the expectations were lowered in college prep courses once AP and IB courses were available. Trust the preparation and expectations you have already provided early in their careers to continue to guide students through OMS. Students of color over-populated college prep courses for a variety of reasons, some individual and some structural but mostly a combination of both. But they also enrolled in these courses, because they perceived they were easier and that they as students were not considered capable or interested in something more challenging. As an academic high school, carry equally high expectations of all students into all classrooms.

Recognize Structural Barriers

Students indicated that they dealt with a variety of structural barriers that impacted their academic decisions. Consider how structural barriers, like socioeconomics and educational background influence students' course taking decisions. In many cases, what teachers read as disinterest is symptomatic of students' very real struggle to manage the stress of home, work, and school.

Openly Discuss the Role That Racial Identity Plays in the Educational Decisions Made by Students, Parents, Teachers, and Administrators

This is the easiest suggestion to make and the most difficult to follow, however, I think asking questions about the role racial idenity plays in educational decisions made by students, parents, teachers, and administrators simply and without judgment can change the outcomes for students in schools. Those students, parents, and staff that were brave enough to answer when I asked are the reason I have anything to offer. It might be helpful to bring in someone from outside the school who can help facilitate these kinds of conversations.

I fully acknowledge that these recommendations are easier said than done. I firmly believe, however, that local level change in schools where policy is practiced can significantly improve the access to opportunities for all students.

INDEX